The Spiritual Laws of

PROSPERITY

Maggy Whitehouse

A *Tree of Life* Book

Text copyright © Maggy Whitehouse 2009
Cover image © Maggy Whitehouse 2009

The moral right of the author has been asserted

All rights reserved.
No part of this publication may be reproduced,
stored in a retrieval system or transmitted, in any
form or by any means, without the prior permis-
sion in writing of the publisher, nor be circulated
in any form of binding or cover other than that in
which it is published and without a similar condition including this condition being imposed on the
subsequent purchaser.

A CIP catalogue record for this book is available
from the British Library

ISBN: 978-1-905806-

Printed and bound in the UK by DG3 London.
DG3 holds the environmental ISO14001
accreditation.

Tree of Life Publishing
Birmingham, UK

CONTENTS

INTRODUCTION

All poverty is first experienced in the soul
Sarah Ban Breathnach.

The great American mystic Joseph Campbell said you could tell the focus of a society by the height of its buildings.

Up until a century ago, churches and temples were the tallest buildings. Then administration took over. Now our great monuments are dedicated to commerce and economics.

These monuments are dedicated to our greatest gods—and our greatest demons. As we will see, humanity has many gods and, any time we put these graven images before our own inner truth then we are setting ourselves up for discomfort.

Everyone faces his or her own issues with money but those on a spiritual quest have the harder task as they seek to make peace with the issue of God and Mammon. In simple truth, there is no conflict: the Source is the source of all including financial prosperity, it is us who make the choices that lead to the results that we are experiencing—but that is not what we have been taught.

Money was invented by humanity; it is a purely imaginative thing fuelled by belief. We have come to see it as a source of evil, inequality and as a power in its own right and we have lost the ability to understand it as a natural resource responding to peace and trust at the soul level. Most of us have been told that we have to 'work for money' without understanding what that actually means. If you work *for* money then you are working for an external acknowledgment of value. You are working for Mammon and not for yourself. Tough words and I'm sorry ... but the causes of both prosperity and poverty are rooted in self-esteem. That's *self*-esteem rather than 'what other people value you at' esteem.

As a teacher of prosperity consciousness for more than a decade I see many clients who are paralysed by fear over money issues. This is not the *feeling* of fear—that is a passing sensation from the ego—but a deep, soul-based emotion that is ingrained, perhaps even over lifetimes.

The great spiritual teacher, Louise Hay, once responded with a sharp intake of breath when I told her I taught prosperity. She said she would rather teach relationships any time over prosperity as people had so much resistance to it.

Just call me a masochist!

The main issue is this: if the soul is activated, as in the spiritual seeker, it must seek union with the Divine. And for century after century (in the Christian world at least), religious teachings have been interpreted to imply that the holy and the good must be poor. Mix this up with aeons of wealth within the Church itself and the promise of 'jam tomorrow' in heaven—*if* you're good enough and don't complain—and you have the basis of mixed and contradictory emotion in the soul.

Each human soul *knows* that it is precious and rare and sacred to the Divine. And yet the teachings of holiness appear to say that it must experience lack in an abundant world. The modern ego is trained not to be selfish but it is rarely taught to be self-full in order to support the soul's sacred quest.

Judaism, Islam and the other major world religions have their own soul issues to contend with but it is Christianity (especially in the UK) which carries the worst confusion over money. Even if you would not call yourself a Christian in any way, if you have been raised in a nominally Christian country, the financial/spiritual programming of centuries will still have a profound affect on your psyche. Remember the Jesuit saying, 'Give me a child until he is seven and I will give you the man.' What we learn at home, at school and from our peers in our childhood will remain as programming forever unless we take conscious steps to change it.

We give to charity; we give to our children; we give whatever we can in order both to be kind and to be good. We pay out on the bills and the house and the car and the credit cards as a priority every month. And because we neglect the call of our soul we give from an empty hand and our soul weeps in consternation at our fear of lack, which we must hide from others because it might be viewed as a judgment from on high because we are not good enough.

There is no reason whatsoever for poverty in this abundant world. The issue is distribution, not lack. But spiritually, it needs to be understood that distribution comes from *us,* not from *them*. By the Law of Cause and Effect, also known as karma and the Law of Attraction, it is our energetic vibration that decides whether we are prosperous or not. It's not what *they* told us, it's what we believe about what they told us. And that can be changed.

Imagine if you had three gifts to give to three people. You walk into the room where they were and one person was bright and excited at the idea of a gift, the second was suspicious or unwilling to trust you and the third said they didn't want anything and you should give it to the needy, you would find it easy to give to the first one and challenging to give to the last two. If the same thing happened several times, it would be quite normal for you to feel the urge to give to the first person only. The second person would be too much like hard work and often you had to leave the gift ungiven and the third, who was trying to make you do something that wasn't what you wanted or planned to do, would just feel so confusing that it's likely that the gift would be dropped or spoilt or broken in the tug of energy.

That's how it must feel for the Source when it tries to give. You can't give something to someone who won't receive it, especially if they believe that you are the one who wrote the rule book on exactly *why* they shouldn't receive it!

The Spiritual Laws of Prosperity, a sister book to *The Little Book of Prosperity* and *From Credit Crunch to Pure Prosperity,* aims to set the record straight on cosmic, divine law when it comes to our health, wealth and happiness. It attempts to show that spiritual law *is* all about living abundantly and that it is centuries of misinterpretation that have misled and restricted us.

It *is* clear always that we must guard against being possessed by our belongings (that is such an interesting word: possessions!) so that we are trapped in a life ruled by 'shoulds' and 'things' instead of being free to go and do what our soul desires. To work at the level of the soul requires discernment and loving kindness—to yourself and to others. Certainly you must have what is beautiful and useful in your life but spiritual growth requires the cutting out of the dead wood so that the beauty can flourish.

It is clear in every spiritual teaching—including Christianity—that abundance is our birthright and everything else is resistance.

To learn to be a magnet for wealth is *not* a selfish thing for the spiritual seeker. It is a service to the world and all the people in it. You cannot teach abundance to others if you, yourself, live in lack. It is clear that giving and giving and giving to others does not solve the world's problems. What will solve them is teaching prosperity consciousness and trust in the abundance of a loving Source Energy (whatever you want to call it).

Embrace prosperity consciousness; teach it on and watch the people of this planet respond with joy. This is the world we seek and it is good.

ON HAPPINESS AND MISERY

*I don't think of all the misery, but of all the beauty
that still remains.*
Anne Frank.

*Regardless of how many boats you send to other
shores or how many ships arrive upon your
shores, you, yourself are an island, separated by
its own pains, secluded in its happiness.'*
Kahlil Gibran.

U nhappy people cause all of the trouble in the
world.

Unhappy people spread sorrow and grief like
influenza, whether it's small-scale within their
homes and families or on an enormous scale
like war. No truly happy person could ever find
themselves in a situation where they were even
partially responsible for a war.

Happy people don't get into debt. Having been
horribly in debt I know through experience that
the one thing guaranteed to get you out of debt is
following your bliss and being happy. That's a big
one, I know. Debt is like disease—not only have
you got to deal with the thought-forms that got you
into the situation in the first place, you have to deal
with the physical reality too.

I got into debt by denying that I was unhappy. I
allowed a feeling of low-grade misery to pervade
everything without even knowing that I was doing
it. In my case the main culprit was pride. I wasn't

going to admit that I might have made any wrong decisions so I wasn't going to allow myself to put them right.

It didn't hurt much; after all, I was fairly used to being miserable. Most of us are. We think it's normal. The debt mounted up because I was seeking happiness but I was seeking it externally and, dammit, that never works!

It is our right — and our spiritual calling — to be happy. Because happiness, too, can spread like influenza. The word 'influenza' simply means 'influence', it doesn't have to mean anything bad.

Unhappy people often find a small amount of happiness helping other unhappy people to feel better. But truthfully, you can't help someone be happy unless you know and understand happiness yourself. Anything else is a temporary relief rather than true healing. It may be a bandage for the soul but it is reliant on the person who tied the bandage to return and help again. That leads to co-dependency and that can never bring happiness.

Ultimately, it's our own unhappiness that we need to sort out. It would be easy to say 'Who *doesn't* want to be happy?' but the truth is that most of us are so busy trying to make everyone else happy that we don't notice the yawning breach inside until it starts yelling through a broken marriage, a broken leg or a broken heart. And then we say, 'But I took care of them! But I was a good husband/wife! But I did my best!'

One clue on whether we have unacknowledged unhappiness is whether we are willing to be alone or unoccupied. The French physicist Blaise Pascal wrote: 'I have discovered that all human evil comes from this, man's being unable to sit still in a room.' Given that when Pascal lived, in the seventeenth

century, there was no TV, very few books to read—
certainly very few novels—no telephones (let
alone no mobile phones) and no DVDs, imagine
how little distraction there was from people's own
thoughts. Nowadays we have so much to distract
us; so many things to *do* that we can run around in
ever-decreasing circle doing 'urgent' stuff to hide
our discontent. Often, we are completely oblivious
to what we are doing or how we feel underneath
because we never have quiet time that would give
our pain a chance to talk to us.

This may seem to be an odd way to start a
book on the spiritual laws of prosperity but it is
unacknowledged feelings of unhappiness that
cause us to get out of synchronisation of our own
abundance in the first place. If we can just learn to
identify and value our own happiness; to pursue it;
to allow it and to revel in it, then we will prosper.
We have to; it's Universal Law.

ABUNDANCE ABOUNDS

This planet is a naturally abundant place; it *works*.
Every day the sun comes up; the Earth turns, the
winds blow, the clouds form and drop the rain, the
seasons come and go. Yes, things change—ice ages
come; heat waves come; there are earthquakes as
the planet sneezes and scratches itself. But they are
all in the natural order of things.

   The main thing that causes any of these events to
speed up or go out of synchronisation in any way at
all is because we humans are unhappy.

   This planet is a living being; it is affected by our
thoughts and feelings as well as what we do. The
nature of the Universe is that it is supported by love;
by joy; by appreciation. That's why angels sing to

the Creative Force—not because It demands their allegiance but for the sheer joy of assisting in the process of creation; of experiencing the expansion of the Multiverse.

Luckily for us, abundance abounds and every moment of love or happiness is a hundred-thousand times more powerful than every moment of discord. If that were not the case, this planet would have self-destructed within a year of the advent of soap operas on television.

What we do physically also has an effect. But happy people don't over-consume; don't abuse drink or drugs, don't live on junk food; don't follow fundamentalist regimes; don't try to control other people's beliefs. All of those are ways to placate the howling of an unhappy ego that has to drug itself or needs to belong to a tribe in order to feel remotely safe.

Happy people don't hate money or the wealthy people who seem to have what they have not. Happy people are just happy. And guess what? They have enough of everything—enough to be able to give stuff away as well.

It's how we react to others' good fortune or how we react to stories of therapies that cost a lot of money that are the tell-tale signs as to whether our own, personal, money situation is trying to get our attention and point out to us the unacknowledged pain.

MONEY TALKS

As I was writing this book I talked to an elegant Ayurvedic doctor about Reiki healing. This lady, who is highly knowledgeable in her field and who appears calm and relaxed, had a complete hissy fit as soon as Reiki was mentioned. She was still angry at how much Reiki used to cost ($10,000 for Mastership about 20 years ago) and threw all sorts of accusations at the system itself which were all associated with her own negative views about money. There was nothing that was good about Reiki as far as she was concerned and never could be. When I said that sometimes Reiki training is now sold for practically nothing she said, 'Well it's useless anyway. *I* wouldn't consider having it.'

There wasn't going to be a positive answer in her mind or even a consideration that perhaps sometimes Reiki training was good and other times it was not so good. And yet, she would never for one moment have believed that her issue was with money itself. It turned out that she had once wanted to train as a Reiki healer and hadn't had sufficient money to do it. Had she been a truly happy person she would have let the matter go after all this time. She wouldn't have been at all bothered at how much people paid to learn Reiki—or whether it worked or not. It would have been up to those people to decide for themselves.

Our wounds always show up when it comes prosperity. Or to be more accurate, when it comes to money. Then the pain shows clearly, both in how we think and speak of money and those who have it. And it shows, too, in how money responds to us. Money, as you know if you've been to any of my workshops, is totally imaginary. It is a means of acknowledging exchange invented by humans. Once it was a token of an amount of gold kept in somewhere like Fort Knox. As the pieces of paper denoting payment moved around, the actual gold was sectioned up appropriately. Now, there often isn't even a piece of paper—and there is certainly no gold behind it.

Money only exists because people believe in it.

When we have a crisis of faith about money, it vanishes into the ether.

If you believe in what the world tells you about money, then you will experience what the rest of the world is experiencing. If you know that it is purely energy and that you are honour-bound by your duty as a human being to focus on happiness, then the external world can have no detrimental, financial effect on you at all.

Wow. That's something, isn't it?

It's easy to say of course. It took me years to achieve it. And even when it *is* achieved, there are times when you may forget for a moment, a day or a week, how to be happy. Shit happens, as they say. It's how we react to it that matters and none of us alive on this planet are immune to death, loss or dramatic change. But once we understand that we are *meant* to recover from the pain; *meant* to seek joy; *meant* to come through happier than ever and *meant* to be prosperous at all levels, even the difficult times are bearable. The Jewish proverb made famous by Abraham Lincoln, 'this, too, shall pass', encourages us to make the most of every happy moment and to realise that the nasty times will also fade away.

The only reason that most people in holistic work attract difficult times is because of the low-grade misery that we don't even notice. After all, we know about positive thinking; we know about the Life Force. Surely we should be happy and prosperous? But the Law of Attraction must respond to our thoughts and feelings and even a slow build-up of negativity can result in quite a surprising landslide when the tipping point is reached.

IN THE BEGINNING...

A certain amount of low-grade misery is trained
into us in early childhood. When we first emerge
into this world we are beings of pure joy who let
the world know very clearly when we are not being
treated as we think we should be! But pretty soon
we learn what behaviour is acceptable and what
is not and that we can't please all the people all
of the time—but that we should keep on trying.
We must let *them* be selfish and have what they
want but we must not be selfish ourselves. Some
people turn into rebels and ostentatiously do what
will make them appear strange to others (which
can lead to unacknowledged loneliness) and
others become people-pleasers (which can lead to
unacknowledged resentment).

We all have a basic make-up—a blueprint if you
like. I use astrology to assess a person's blueprint
although I always try to make it clear that we all
have free will. We have the ability to overcome
our astrology with consciousness; it's simply the
default position.

So we all have a default position—and we have
training from our parents, teachers, brothers and
sisters, outer family and our peers. We learn very
young what behaviour is acceptable and what is
not and what gets us attention. Getting attention
is generally perceived as being a good thing by
a healthy psyche as it means we are likely to be
fed and looked after. For a psyche damaged by
abuse, whether physical or psychological, getting
attention is generally perceived as a bad thing.

Our ego—the lower part of our psyche—is our
natural, everyday thinks-on-automatic aspect. It is
designed to protect us it will reinforce our survival
instinct. Therefore, if we are repressed and we

never became the pianist/actor/singer we wanted to be because we had to do what our parents and siblings needed us to do, we are likely to dislike other people who are successful. It's called projection and it's rarely conscious.

We also have a subconscious 'place in the tribe'—the pecking order if you like. Until my husband and I had chickens I didn't realise that the pecking order was a definite and powerful thing. To start with, Wiz was the lead hen; she was the one with the most feathers (they are ex-battery hens) and the most adventurous. Then Fan became lead hen because she grew stronger fastest. But then she hurt her foot and both Wiz and Phyl (previously the bottom of the heap) leapt up the food chain and bossed her around.

My husband summed up the kind of childhood both he and I had with the story of how, when he went to a friend's house, he was instructed not to be selfish, to watch what they wanted to watch on the TV and not to ask to watch his favourite show. But when the friends came round to his house, they were encouraged to watch their favourite show because they were the guests… If you can relate to that in any way, it could be a root cause of poverty consciousness.

RELIGION AND BELIEF

We become miserable because we are trained to think that we don't matter and that deep inside we are alone with our fears our faults and our resentments. We believe that our limited experience of ourselves (reflected back from other people) constitutes our whole nature. And somehow, we are *wrong*.

Even if you aren't a Christian, if you were raised

in a nominally Christian country, you will have been encouraged to fear some external being called *God* who sacrificed His own son because of our sins. We don't remember that somewhere within us resides a supreme being of peace; we fear that God is out there and if He'll do something that mean to His own son *what is he going to do to us?*

Belief in a totally external God can only lead to fear and despair. Even in the New Age, where we speak of Source, Chi, the Universe, Goddess or Unity, we are slightly avoiding the issue. We don't speak of God because we fear God. We can deal with Source because it is neutral and has no Gospel. We see *God* as the external judge. And Jesus of Nazareth was someone who lived a life of poverty and who gave his life for others. If we want any love from God, we must do the same.

Oh, ouch.

I'm not a big fan of St. Augustine but he hit the nail right on the head when he wrote: 'Our whole business in life is to restore to health the eye of the heart whereby God may be seen.' That's the *real* God; the great Joygiver who wants nothing more than our happiness. Not the nasty, mean brute that we have come to believe in from misunderstood scriptural teachings perpetuated by a priesthood that doesn't understand itself—and sometimes doesn't even believe.

In the last century in particular, with the advent of worldwide news and science, we have lost the idea that we are naturally happy and abundant beings. We think that happiness is somehow a matter of chance, such as winning the lottery. Or that we have to work hard to earn enough money and *then* we will have suffered enough to deserve to be happy. Or that if we take care of everyone else at the expense of ourselves, then we will deserve to be happy.

But you can't get to happiness on a road filled with suffering. The Law of Attraction doesn't work like that.

Luckily, people like Esther Hicks with the Teachings of Abraham, Eckhart Tolle, Louise Hay and Deepak Chopra are here to remind us; but if you, like me, have layers of trained thinking to dissolve you may have to make an effort to rediscover your own happiness. Not a painful effort; not something which is a struggle but what Liz Gilbert, in her wonderful book *Eat, Pray, Love* (Penguin), calls 'diligent joy.' We have to re-member our happiness.

The idea of this book is to address the great spiritual *laws* of this planet—all of which are aspects of the Law of Attraction—in the hope of helping the inner child in us all to understand that we have a right to strive for happiness. It is not a selfish inclination; it is not 'wrong', it is our spiritual duty.

There are examples from Judaism, Christianity, Islam, Buddhism, Shinto, Hinduism, Atheism—you name it, it's got teachings on how very, very important it is to harness the Law of Attraction (though it's more usually referred to as the Law of Karma). That darn Law works whatever we do so we might as well turn it to our—and our loved-ones'—advantage.

Oddly enough, if you examine all the spiritual teachings of the world (including the ones that initially make it look as if God is a total bastard) you'll find that they are originally intended to be guidance as to how the Law of Attraction works.

As the great prosperity teacher Dr. Catherine Ponder, author of *The Dynamic Laws of Prosperity*

(DeVors) and dozens of other books, writes, it's not so much 'fear of the Lord' that is the beginning of wisdom. It's 'fear of the *Law*'. And before you say 'I don't think we should be afraid of anything', I bet you would be afraid of a raging fire! The Law of Attraction is just like fire. It is a wonderful servant but it will rampage out of control unless we learn how to live happily. And, surprisingly enough, the world's spiritual laws will help us to do just that.

Perhaps, however, it is easier to explain that the Hebrew word used for 'fear' in the original Old Testament quotation is *yirah*, which also means 'awe', 'respect' and 'reverence'.

I am very happy to live with awe, respect and reverence for the Law of Attraction. It is so simple and so pure. I hope this book will help you feel the same way.

EXERCISE ONE:
Set your intention.

Tomorrow is a new day, you shall begin it well and serenely.
Ralph Waldo Emerson.

All spiritual practices include ritual that signify a drawing in, or down, of good. Ceremonies of some kind have been conducted by humanity since the beginning of time and many of them are so old that it seems that the angelic forces, the Universe and the Earth know them by heart. I only have to start one of the services I facilitate in the independent sacramental church into which I am ordained and I am almost drowned out by the chorus of energy that knows, supports and builds the aim of the ritual much better than I do.

Rituals set an intent and, if your intention is to become happier and more prosperous, then it's good to have a regular practice that enforces that idea in your mind and in the annals of the Universe. Throughout the book there will be ideas and exercises for you to follow but the most important of all is the idea of the Law of First Intention.

Even the Bible starts off with 'in the beginning.'

Start the day with a prayer of intent. It doesn't have to be any more than, 'Let this be a good day' or 'I want to be happy today.' If your first conscious thought to the Universe is one that moves you forward towards your desires it can start to get a momentum going.

Simple things are best as they won't over-challenge you.

If you read *The Little Book of Prosperity* you'll know that I started to wear the perfume called 'Joy' when I was getting divorced. At first the irony of that amused me and then I realised how reinforcing it was of what I wanted. Now I have a bottle of 'Joy' on my work desk and the first thing I do on sitting down at my desk in the morning is to dab my neck and wrists with Joy. Then I light a tea-light candle and, if the desk needs tidying, I put it into a little more order.

If I do that before I open my computer to write or to check my emails, I have set a clear intention that I want the day to be joyous, spiritual and organised.

What intentions can you set for your day? Whatever it is, it needs to be done with *consciousness*. Know you are doing it and why you are doing it.

Hint: if doing something that used to make you

21

feel good has lost its power, or even makes you think 'why hasn't it happened yet?' the energy has changed and you need to find something new to do. Changing and updating simple rituals is important. The great and ancient ones don't need it so much because they are built on a structure that builds energy towards a positive goal. Simple rituals need to work for you *now*.

THE LAW OF ATTRACTION — THE LAW OF NATURAL ABUNDANCE.

Expect your every need to be met. Expect the answer to every problem, expect abundance on every level...
Eileen Caddy, Findhorn founder.

Whatever we are waiting for—peace of mind, contentment, grace, the inner awareness of simple abundance—it will surely come to us, but only when we are ready to receive it with an open and grateful heart.
Sarah Ban Breathnach.

If you are feeling depressed there is nothing more annoying than someone trying to cheer you up with a load of positive thinking.

I remember a builder yelling at me, 'cheer up love! It might never happen', two days after my first husband died. I replied, 'It already has,' to which that bright spark quipped, 'Well there's nothing to worry about then is there!'

It's a vibrational thing. How we feel dictates the range of vibration we can experience. At that point I really, *really* wasn't anywhere near being able to see the bright side of life so the builder infuriated me. But oddly enough, that's the point.

Before he called out to me, I was in depression — despair. As I reacted to his words, I felt fury and rage. I didn't realise it at the time but actually those emotions were slightly more positive. The builder might have been irritatingly cheerful but he had pulled me energetically towards a better vibration. In that case it was just too much for me to be able to move with it and sustain the new feeling and I had too much ego-social training to allow myself rage. Had I understood the Law of Attraction in those days I might have been able to flow that fury through me and move on to the next level of anger and then, perhaps, to frustration and onwards to hope. As it was, I couldn't trust my feelings to be the right ones and I just sank back into depression.

The Teachings of Abraham (www.abraham-hicks.com) talk of the levels of emotion with which we can resonate. If we're depressed, we can relate to despair, rage, revenge, anger, discord, sadness, irritation and frustration. We avoid bright, bouncy people and TV programmes and grumble about them along the lines of 'they're no better than they should be' or 'Yes it may look good now but just you wait…'

If we are happy we avoid people expressing the angry or depressive emotions whenever we can because they just feel terrible. We can, however, resonate with joy, laughter, kindness, giving, compassion, nostalgia and a little, gentle regret as long as it's got a positive side too.

As we feel any of these emotions, we move along a sliding scale with each thought we experience building up a bigger picture and taking us along a path either towards or away from positivity.

It's often hard for us to make that move from depression to rage—women, particularly, have been trained that anger is an unpleasant emotion. But you only have to see the soap operas where hatred, anger and revenge are acted out for us every night of the week to see that our subconsciouses are calling out for a shift from our misery to something better. Vicarious vibrational movement via the TV is all very well but we also have to do it for ourselves. When my second marriage ended, I found (temporary) great help and support in the *Terminator 3* movie when I found myself yelling 'die you bitch!' along with the heroine. But I had to get out to my punch bag with a broom handle to get the emotion fully out!

Please understand that I am not advocating taking real revenge—or taking a broom handle to the other person. The Law of Attraction is clear that it is never the other person that's the issue. The issue is how *you* attracted their behaviour into your life. But letting go of the pressure within you (in safe ways) is a very important step. Louise Hay (*You Can Heal Your Life,* Hay House*)* suggests thumping pillows or digging holes and sounding off your anger into those before covering them over. If you don't think you're angry (a common blockage in spiritual people) try it anyway and just pretend to be cross. After a while the real thing will turn up; it was just hiding behind your 'nice person' persona.

There were probably quite a few exploding turtles on a certain beach in Tobago after my first boyfriend following Henry's death dumped me on a paradise holiday there. I discovered, as I dug hole after hole in the beach, exactly how angry I was with so many other people and circumstances in my life. Fortunately, I learned healing pretty soon after and realised that it might be a good idea to send some blessings to that beach to transmute my dumped negative energy. But at least I'd moved on to anger from depression!

25

In general, our thoughts think us rather than the other way around. They creep into our heads and chatter away whether we want them to or not and, all too often, they re-infect themselves without our giving them a single conscious moment of attention.

But one thing works to cheer everyone up, even if it's only a little: going outside on a lovely day and spending some time with nature.

Why? Because of the naturally positive vibration of that natural environment. Nature is the ultimate demonstration of the Law of Attraction. Abundance abounds. Haven't you noticed that spring *happens every year?* Even with all the doom and gloom expressed over global warming (which doesn't help it, obviously) the seasons still come and go; roses and peonies still bloom; autumn comes and the leaves fall to fertilise the soil for another year.

The Earth will heal herself. She is quite capable and willing to do so if needs be. In a worst-case scenario, all she has to do to get rid of the irritations on her surface is to erupt a few times. Then she can get back to being pollution-free in a couple of million years or so. She doesn't compute time like us; she doesn't worry about ice-ages or droughts. It's all just a series of natural cycles to her and if there's something pesky that's getting up her nose, she'll get rid of it in her own time.

We, on the other hand, want to sort it out *right now*. Have you ever stopped to think how arrogant and how controlling that might be? Let's stop those dirty polluters (who strangely enough seem to be the corporate, rich people—have you noticed? What a good opportunity to project our negative feelings about money). So we set up campaigns of hostility against the people who are upsetting us instead of realising that we do way more energetic harm to the planet through our hatred than they do through their petrol fumes.

A lot of campaigns to save the planet, save the whales, save the rainforest etc. are fuelled through anger and loathing towards others. Not a helpful vibration. Those campaigners who are actively seeking solutions are wonderful beings but those who focus on the problems are working against their deepest desire for healing. I once had a much-loved framed picture of dolphins which was underlined with the sad phrase, *Endangered Species*. One morning I woke up and looked at it and realised with acute shock that it was saying quite clearly *End Angered Species!* What a message we can put out without realising it!

It's so easy to blame money and the people who have it because this is a visible, external aspect of our own inner discomfort. We do harm to ourselves through any hostile vibration we project and, as we hate money, guess what? It will avoid us like the plague we say it is.

We have to learn that it's never them. It's always us.

One more time with feeling, please: It's *never* them. It's *always* us.

If we were as balanced as we would like to be, firstly *they* wouldn't be anywhere in our consciousness—they wouldn't be able to touch us emotionally. And secondly, if we were all happy and balanced, then there would be no problems anyway. We either solve the problem through our own self-development or we *are* the problem through our own inner resentments and the low-grade miseries that our minds don't even register.

The natural law of abundance is always there to

help. The only thing we need to do to observe and to feel it is to take time out.

You cannot fully appreciate the nature of a rose by one glance. You have to savour its colour, its texture, its scent. You can't absorb the refreshing energy of a fountain, a waterfall or a stream unless you take a moment to relax or sit or lie beside it and breathe in its rhythm.

We should probably get onto tree-hugging as well. I'm not a rabid tree-hugger but I must admit I've cuddled a few in my time. Very honest beings, trees. The first one I ever hugged was when I was on a New Age trip where I was told to go hug a tree. I chose a rather hunky Sycamore and threw my arms around it.

'Go away and leave me alone,' it said quite clearly.

If you spend time relaxing around a tree and *then* hug it, you generally get a better response. And if you ask it to help you with some healing energy, you will get a better response yet but if, like I did, you just throw your energy at it in the complete illusion that you are there to heal the tree you may get a surprise.

As a general rule, gardeners are less crazy than the rest of us. Not only do they spend a lot of time with nature but they understand about weeds. For a garden to flourish there must be some weeding done. Our destructive thoughts are like bindweed or ground elder. If we leave just a little bit behind, it will all grow up again and it will try to throttle the good and the beautiful.

It's a rare soul that can eliminate all that is unhelpful—but it is our spiritual task to keep the weeds at a minimum.

Gardeners also understand that a weed is simply

a plant that you don't want around. You don't need to have that particular plant banned; you just make sure that there aren't any in *your* garden.

To take the metaphor further, if you are living next to a house with an overgrown garden and their weeds blow over or climb under to infect your garden, then that's an indication of the vibration of the company you keep energetically. Focusing on your own weeding is even more important as that will change your vibration.

Even if this is a literal truth then weeding and cultivating your own patch will change the energy around you. If you are positive or neutral about what you are doing then the careless neighbours will either have to change themselves or move away.

However, if you fuss and fret about their weeds and how they mess you up, then energetically you are calling them into your own space—and more will come. Abraham-Hicks sums this up by saying the vibration becomes 'Come to me this thing that I do not want.' Your attention on *anything* draws that vibration to you.

The more you do this work, the more true that becomes as you hone your vibration. When life is generally a mess, more mess doesn't make much difference but, when you are clearing and sorting, a little bit of extra mess really hits the vibrational shock button!

Of course, somehow you attracted that mess (and how irritating is that?) but almost certainly it will have been something to which your consciousness was oblivious.

Gardeners also know that everything grows in its season—and dies. Death is a natural consequence of life and, before medical science came along, people were much more at peace with that. Nowadays, we think that any death before the age of 80+ is somehow wrong. It is not. Just like some plants are throttled by weeds, some fall on barren ground or some are scorched by the sun, some people die young. It is a fact of life, as is grief.

In the old days, pre-science, we used to believe more in the afterlife; the ancestors and reincarnation; we knew that we would see and experience the loved ones again. It may not help, immediately, to know that your beloved has suddenly remembered how to fly and been reunited with other deeply-loved souls from aeons past but there is a feeling of rightness to it along with the grief.

The secular world doesn't know or believe any of this and consequently fights against all aspects of loss.

Nowadays someone has to be blamed for things that go wrong—from global warming to the death of loved a one. Blame is sometimes good and sometimes bad. If it's a vibrational step up from feeling anguish, helplessness and despair then it's a better vibration on the way towards frustration and hope. We prefer the feeling of blame to the feeling of guilt because it's an active vibration rather than a passive one; you can feel the difference within yourself if you speak of guilt or blame. However, blame needs to be a step towards a better feeling rather than a place of habit because, if it becomes the norm in our life, we will never move on to a vibration where blame is not necessary.

Of course we hate to lose those we love. But love is never lost; never wasted.

When Henry died, I was a magazine writer and managed (even without knowledge of the Law of Attraction) to get myself commissioned to write an article on people who had found new love within a year of the death of a life-partner.

The majority of people I found to interview were male — women take longer to move on as a general rule. But two aspects were very striking. Firstly, I interviewed Colin Murray Parkes, psychiatrist and life-president of *Cruse*, the Bereavement Care organisation, who told me from his own experience that those who had genuinely loved, fell in love again within a few years of loss.

Conversely, the people who seem to mourn for years and never find a good reason to thrive again quite often had not been happy in their marriage... and it was possible that they subconsciously built up the idea of loss as an excuse not to love again because it hurt too much last time.

Of course it was quite possible that the pain of loss was too much to be able to consider going through such agony again but, apparently, it's more a question of whether the relationship was considered worth the pain at the end. In my case, I was already saying 'It was worth it.' I would never have wanted not to have loved Henry and been loved in return even though it was for such a very short time.

Secondly, much to my surprise, I fell in love again and was married for a second time within two years of Henry's death.

Over the years I have been able to use Dr. Murray Parkes' words to comfort several people who were bereaved. And all of them were deeply heartened, even though at the time they didn't want to love again. The words were also very useful for a friend who was perplexed and upset when his recently widowed father announced that he was going to marry his wife's best friend. The friend had thought

31

that an indication that his Dad couldn't have loved his Mum when the opposite was true.

Pet owners discover this too—you think when you lose a beloved dog or cat that the grief will never end. But once the first shafts of pain have dissolved, a wriggling puppy or kitten will swiftly capture the heart that yearns to love again as it loved before. You'll probably love the next pet more because you understand love more fully. Isn't it somehow heartening to know that there will always be more and more love to come?

Incidentally, I used to hate the idea of a pet being lonely after death. That was just the fear of my ego—who's to say the pet had only ever been just my pet in just one incarnation? But it added to the pain.

I found great comfort from Michael Newton's *Destiny of Souls* (Llewellyn) where it is made beautifully clear that animal souls are not ego-driven or overwhelmed by identity issues as we are. They accept and blend with their environment, rather than fighting to control it, so they can return very happily to a kind of group soul of their species. However when we, or any other beloved owner, is discarnate we can call them to come to us and spend however much time with us we chose and the individual domesticated animal can, and will, come.

It's also obvious, when we have an animal in our care, that they don't worry about dying. They never even think about it until it happens and then they just go. It is the ego that fears dying because it dies with the body. The self and soul go on. An animal doesn't have an ego in the same way as a human does (have you *ever* heard of an animal worrying whether it's bum looked big?).

I've never personally owned a dog that didn't die

32

naturally. As each one grew old, I used to whisper to her 'live long and happily; die peacefully in your sleep.' But then I never had a dog before I knew about the Law of Attraction.

So, summing up: Abundance abounds. The Universe and the Earth work perfectly: our planet breathes in; it breathes out. It can adjust itself by moving its plates and letting off steam in earthquakes and volcanoes and its seasons follow one another as they should.

Yes, human beings die in accidents and earthquakes; we die in automobiles and aircraft. But we also die in accidents with vending machines and mattresses. We die when we are due to die and, if they truly loved us, those we loved have the ability to love again even more deeply.

It's very simple. No one ever said it was easy.

However, just knowing that abundance abounds makes it easier to understand that we can align with it whatever our circumstances. That's why spiritual teachers recommend meditation. If we can just still our mind from the chatter, grief and care, then the Universe takes us gently into its hand and moves us forwards with the natural abundance. That's what 'Let go and let God' actually means. Let the Earth, the planets and the stars carry you in their care. They will take you to good places because they don't know any other reality.

EXERCISE TWO
Stilling or calming the mind.

The human mind is not used to being still; we feed it with news, the Internet, telephones, TV etc. etc. But just five minutes a day of peacefulness with a still or just a slowly-moving mind, is enough to get the Universe conspiring in our favour.

Meditation is a required discipline. It's simple and it works. Try it. Two minutes a day is a good start; you can even do that on a bus or tube train (though not in the driving seat of a car!). If stilling the mind is too hard do a little, gentle visualisation about a lovely holiday you once had or hope to have. Just that couple of minutes every day is enough to get you flowing with the natural stream of abundance and, hopefully, it will soon feel so good that you can't imagine life without it.

If there are any meditation classes near you, do enrol and go whenever you can. Don't worry that you can't meditate to start with; that you spend most of the time trying not to get cramp or your mind wanders frantically. You won't be the only one in that group doing or feeling just the same! Committing to meditation is a sad challenge for the ego but, if you persevere, it will come to accept and even like it. It will start to accept the relaxed energy from others and submit with grace.

I only learnt to meditate properly because I went on a course that required meditation and journaling every morning for six weeks. If I didn't do it, I didn't get the certificate. By the time I'd got to the finish date, my ego was completely re-trained and now it nags at me if I *don't* meditate!

Here are some mantras which may help. A mantra is a word (hopefully with a spiritual meaning!) which you just repeat in your mind over and over again. They are helpful because they give the mind something to do rather than being totally silent.

After a while, you can think behind the mantra — i.e. your mind can wander even though you are saying the words. But it is still easier to bring it back because there is a point of reference.

Judaic mysticism often uses some of the Hebrew

34

letters that form names of the Divine. God is usually known as *Yahveh* which is spelt *YHVH* (Biblical Hebrew has no vowels). The letters are pronounced *Yod Hey Vah Hey*. Whispering these to yourself as a mantra is very calming and therapeutic.

The highest name of God, in Judaism, is *Eheyeh Asher Eheyeh* which means 'I Am that I Am.' All the secrets of existence are said to reside in this name which is so sacred and not to be used without full consciousness and care. It refers to God the transcendent and God the immanent i.e. the great all-encompassing God and the God (Christ) within you. To meditate on this name is to draw each aspect of the Divinity into complete understanding and unity.

It is pronounced as *Ee-high-yah A-share Ee-high-yah*. You can also just pronounce the Hebrew initials for *Eheyeh (AHYH)* pronounced *Aleph-Hey-Yod-Hey*.

There's an even simpler one from Hindu Yogis, *Ham Sah* (pronounce the *Ham as Hhhham*). It means 'I am that' and it's a wonderful example of how all the faiths come from the same root because, as you whisper *Ham Sah, Ham Sah*, you are also saying 'I Am that I Am.'

THE LAW OF CLEANSING

'God dwells within you as you.'
Swami Muktananda.

'You bear God within you, poor wretch, and know it not.'
Epictetus.

'First mend yourself, and then mend others.'
Jewish proverb

It's a tough call being God and most of us would rather not do it. Just think of the responsibility ...

The trouble is, we *are* It. Each of us, individually is a unique and irreplaceable part of the Whole.

The heart of every mystical tradition teaches that God, the Source, the Holy One, the Creative Force, the Christ, whatever you want to call it, lives quite happily right inside you. It's not something you have to go and find, it's something already there.

And as it is abundance personified (or should it be 'deified'?) it is a magnet for all good things.

The true spiritual seeker is the one who wants to find the divine at any cost—even if finding it also brings wealth. Don't panic; you don't have to sit on mountains of cash but you do have to see abundance in all things and quit blaming money and the people who have it for all the world's problems.

Those who only seek God in poverty are missing the point of the Divine altogether. You only have to read a biography of St. Francis of Assisi, who embraced poverty and suffering, to see that his initial impulse to move from senseless hedonism and wealth went wildly out of balance. From living a simple life where he could trust Source to take care of his every need, he moved to virtual starvation and self-immolation, both of which are seriously unhealthy not to mention fanatical. Even when he died, he was still challenging himself to give up more and deny himself even the beauty of the planet to prove his worthiness to God. This kind of story is not surprising in a religion that promotes the idea of the holy martyr. Its root—the story of Jesus—certainly does include one man's painful death but he was on the cross for less time than the average pregnant woman is in labour. Jesus's story is about much, much more than the time of suffering. Even the crucifixion itself is a demonstration that if you surrender and die to the suffering, then resurrection is a done deal.

Let me take you through that in more detail...

Understood metaphysically, the crucifixion is a cleansing process. In each of the four Gospels the story is approached differently, with the two that represent the physical body and the psyche (Matthew and Mark) focusing on the physical and psychological pain. The body and the lower psyche do cry out in anguish and grief when hurt and these are the two Gospels that carry the lines 'Father, why has Thou forsaken me?'

Those lines are not in Luke or John. The spiritual Gospel (Luke) focuses on letting go and forgiving those who hurt Jesus. 'Father, forgive them, they know not what they do.' These are very powerful lines because most of the time the people who hurt us are acting unconsciously. They are so concerned with their own pain and the need to prove themselves right that they are willing to hurt another. And hurting another cannot bring peace, so they are setting up bad experiences for themselves.

The Divine Gospel (John) is about giving up and moving through the pain to let it go. All Jesus says in this book is 'It is done.'

When we are sick or hurt our bodies and psyches are always in discomfort or pain but the 'real' us — the spiritual being — can see that it is our own creation and that all we have to do is give up the need to blame or be right in order to move on. It's not about Jesus doing it *for* us; it's about a holy Anointed One of God demonstrating the levels on which we work and how we too can overcome our most savage of challenges.

Incidentally, there is no evidence at all that Jesus was poor as most Christians are taught. The son of a carpenter in those days was seriously middle-class. Nazareth was just four miles from the great city of Sepphoris which was being re-built after a major fire and the Greek word *tekton,* which is generally translated as carpenter, also included stonemasons who built houses. So the family of a carpenter would have plenty of work.

Even when Jesus chose to be a travelling teacher, these were people who were valued as storytellers. Even as late as the 1980s I saw, first-hand, how highly storytellers in China were valued; the ones I saw never had to ask for a meal or a place to sleep. It's hard for us to realise how popular someone with new information would have been in a world without books, radio, cinema or TV.

As for the story of the stable, there we are right back to St. Francis who invented the story of the cave, the ox and the ass. He was the first one to set up a Christmas crib and we have followed his instructions ever since.

In the Bible, the baby Jesus was certainly laid in a manger but in those days, animals' stables were nearly always attached to the house rather than in a separate building because of the warmth the beasts generated—you can still see this in old villages such as Polopos in southern Spain. Yes it is possible, even likely that if that Joseph and Mary were staying at an inn, there would be separate stables. But there's the rub. The bit that says 'no room for them in the inn' is a misleading translation. The word *kataluma* doesn't mean inn, it means upper room or guest room in a private house. An inn (mentioned in the very same Gospel) is *pandocheion*.

If the Bible story is true and they went to Bethlehem for the census because Joseph was from the town, it's unlikely that he didn't have relatives in Bethlehem and, from my own personal knowledge of Jewish families, it would have been regarded as an insult if he had chosen to stay in an inn rather than with relatives. In a private house that was full of people, Joseph and Mary would certainly have been separated, just as in an inn where you slept in dormitories according to your sex (due to the Jewish purity laws). A woman in labour would want privacy and her blood etc. would be such as to render any other woman in the room with her ritually unclean. So Mary would be much better off in the kitchen/stable area of a private house where there would be space, hot water and straw to help with the mess of childbirth than either in a dormitory or an upper room. And she could have her husband with her if she wanted him.

Jesus never taught that poverty was a good thing, he just thought we should be free enough to do what we truly wanted. After all, the word 'possession' is a two-edged sword. If your house, job and belongings—and the school that your children go to—possess you then you are trapped. A healthy soul can manifest whatever it needs in life and it can move around unimpeded to where it is most valued and *of* most value. No wonder that people keep saying that wealth doesn't bring happiness; it can't if it includes possession as part of the package and if it is only wealth at the ego level (*stuff,* mostly!). Wealth at the level of the soul means you can simply put your hand out and 'ask, believing' to quote Jesus. 'Ask, believing, and it is given.' The believing bit is the key which is often left out in Law of Attraction teachings. The believing is the job of the soul and it requires discipline (also the job of the soul) as in actually doing those affirmations; turning up for the meditation or the workshop and doing the work required instead of reading the book and expecting it to work automatically,

The Buddha got the balance right. He began life wealthy and privileged and tried the way of austerity but found it wanting. He recommended the 'middle way,' which is the one of allowing abundance without unnecessarily pursuing it. Since the mind was connected to the body, he taught that denying the body would hamper concentration, just as overindulgence would distract one from concentration.

Incidentally, on the subject of 'pursuing' the much-loved 23rd Psalm contains the lines, 'Surely goodness and mercy shall follow me all the days of my life and I will dwell in the house of the Lord forever.'

The Hebrew word translated as 'follow' is *radaph* which, more accurately, means 'chase, harass or pursue.' So the psalm is saying that joy and abundance *are chasing after us* with intent and enthusiasm. So if they're not finding us, what's going on? A fourth interpretation of *radaph* is 'put to flight' and that's what we do—we run away from the Divine within because we can't face its glory. It's the ego that runs because to surrender to the Source is just too scary if life is ruled by social, work and family life. After all, we're weird enough for them already, right?

It seems that this particular chapter is going to be choc-a-bloc with quotations but this one from the Gospel of Thomas is a perfect fit: 'If you will not know yourselves, you dwell in poverty and it is you who are that poverty.'

Poverty doesn't *happen* to us. Poverty is *in* us.

But so is Divine Abundance.

THE DIVINE IN THE DEPTHS

Everything we experience is within us.

Spiritual work is often referred to as 'remembering' or as 'peeling off the layers of an onion' to get to the heart of ourselves. We can only do that if we believe that at the heart of ourselves there is something good. If we believe that we are evil to the core, we won't go there—no matter how many holistic workshops we attend or spiritual books that we read.

I got to my inner core for a brief moment at the very beginning of my spiritual search but, even though I've spoken of that moment many times in discussions on grief or despair, it was nearly 20 years before I finally realised what actually happened.

Henry had died just a few weeks earlier and

friends were starting to say 'don't cry' when I wanted to howl, so I was closing in on myself in the grief. I was more than usually miserable one evening so I decided to sit in the bath with a gin and tonic and allow myself the unhappiness, instead of tying it up in a little bag and hiding it in my wardrobe.

I had to push it a bit past the general crying, because my ego was trained to control itself, but pretty soon I was weeping like a waterfall and sinking down and down into the darkness of fear, anguish and loss.

It was a long way down and frightened parts of me kept saying, 'turn round now, Maggy!' but I ignored them and went on digging that hole in my heart and my guts.

After about half an hour, just as I thought I might suffocate from lack of breath, everything stopped. The darkness became spangled with little lights and something gentle touched me with a soothing enquiry and—believe it or not—laughter.

I laughed in my rapidly cooling bath with my empty glass of gin and tonic and I knew that I was totally safe and happy to the core.

It was *me* in there. The Divine Me. Alive and blissful even at the height of my grief. And You are in there, right in the heart of You. It isn't about going to an ashram in India or to visit Deepak Chopra in San Diego (nice though that is), it's about peeling away the coverings to you.

And if it were very, very hard to do, we'd all be doing it. The fact is that it's slow and simple where we want swift and dramatic revelation.

Ah, you may say, what about those who commit suicide? They go down into the darkness of depression and they don't come back laughing.

There are two answers to that. Firstly, how do we know? That final act of despair may bring them to the point of total joy as they become one with the Divine as they transition to a different plane. Admittedly, it took more pain than anyone should ever have to endure to get to that point. Suicides leave terrible pain behind them and the verdict of an inquest in such an event is always 'suicide while the balance of the mind was disturbed.' In such cases, an horrific depression takes hold in a way that makes the suicide genuinely believe that those they love will be better off without them. It also makes them so disconnected from their soul that the only way they can find it again is to die. There are also all sorts of soul-group and karmic issues around suicide.

You are not at that point. If you were, you wouldn't be optimistic enough to read a book on prosperity.

So, the Spiritual Law of Cleansing is about gently wiping away the dirt to reveal the beauty underneath. But the all-important caveat is *are you prepared to find perfection?*

If you feel a bit uncomfortable about that, try not to worry; it does take quite a while to get there. The good news is that, as you get closer, it doesn't seem quite so mad, bad or arrogant. And other people notice that your eyes get clearer and brighter, your posture and health improve, you smile a lot more and your life seems to be working out pretty well. They may even ask you what your secret is.

CLEANSING RITUALS

Most of the world's religions have cleansing rituals, ranging from the orthodox Jewish Mikvah to the Shinto washing of hands and mouth before entering a shrine. In the Mikvah, you wash yourself thoroughly first and then submerge yourself entirely in a pool or bath of clean, naturally-running water. This is a spiritual cleansing and, in an energetic way, similar to taking a plunge bath after a sauna.

In Shinto this particular type of cleansing is called *temizu*, from the Japanese word *imi* which means 'impurities.' The symbol of washing one's hands and mouth before praying is cleansing the impurities from within, pushing out and preventing bad spirits from entering.

There are also thorough full-body cleansing rituals, called *Misogi,* in running water including waterfalls and spas. In addition, all Shinto shrines are hung with straw rope and white paper, both of which are believed to cleanse and transmute negative energies.

Christianity has baptism which happens only once in a lifetime and is believed to cast out the devil (a Christian invention) and cleanse us of sin. However, Catholics cross themselves with holy water on entering a church as a regular cleansing ritual.

Islam also requires cleansing of hands, feet and face before entering a mosque and before touching a copy of the Koran (although there is nothing in the Koran itself to specify this). If water is inappropriate due to sickness or lack, sand is used to cleanse instead.

North American Indians and the Norse faiths use the 'sweat lodge', a kind of sauna, to cleanse themselves in mind, body and soul. A Scandinavian couple going to be married will often both take a sauna to cleanse them for the new start in life.

A lot of these rituals have become demonised as misogynistic, because they include the need for cleansing after menstruation or touching a bleeding woman, but they actually include all 'issues of blood', any kind of sickness and being in the presence of death, whatever your sex. As well as having spiritual significance, hygiene was a matter of life and death for peoples who lived without constant running water and under threat of typhoid, cholera and plague.

But cleansing works on all levels. It can be done physically, psychologically and spiritually. Some traditions use it to exorcise evil spirits and, when it comes down to it, there's not a lot of difference between the idea of an evil spirit and a repetitive negative thought that keeps a human being depressed and unhappy.

As the famous phrase on the mystical emerald tablet of Hermes Trismegistus says, 'As above, so below'. Cleansing is an important process in unravelling the real, prosperous you.

We are all cluttered with unhelpful thoughts, actions and beliefs. Releasing the beliefs is usually the most important because a belief is a thought that has been repeated so many times that it is engraved upon our ego-conciousness. Even if millions of other people believe the same thing, it's only because they have learnt to think that particular thought. It doesn't have to be objectively true.

We believe so many things that hurt us, don't we? The painful emotion that comes when we think or see these 'true' things that are bad come from the soul. It is telling us that we are giving too much attention to the negative and not enough to the positive. Unfortunately, our egos have been trained to believe that feeling bad and continuing to look at the thing that makes us feel bad is a good thing. It's kind to lower your energy in order to relate to others and it's a good thing to focus on unhappiness rather than looking for peace of mind and solutions. If you were God you'd fall over laughing at that one.

Fortunately, we don't need to unravel the unhelpful beliefs one by one — we don't even need to know what they are (although the biggest ones will shout for our attention); we can just cleanse and cleanse and cleanse in a general way.

That's what the world's great prayers asking for forgiveness are meant to be about. Unfortunately, most of them come across as self-accusations of unworthiness, so it's not surprising that either we don't want to say them or we don't believe that there is any good in us whatsoever. Or that there is some great judgemental God out there pointing at us.

The only thing pointing at us is us: our own projections of negativity and lack. We think we are nothing or not good enough when in fact we are pure gold that just happens to be covered over in layers of muck (which we have painted over and varnished to provide some kind of veneer that will fool other people that we are okay).

Jack Canfield tells this story of the Golden Buddha in his *Chicken Soup for the Soul:*

A group of monks from a monastery had to move a clay Buddha to a different temple. But the Buddha was much heavier than expected and when they tried to move it, the clay began to crack. It also started to rain so the abbot had the statue covered with a tarpaulin while he worked out what to do.

Later that evening he went to check on the damage to the Buddha. He shone his torch under the covering to see if it was staying dry but, to his surprise, something shone back at him. Curiously, he knocked away some shards of clay and he found that hidden underneath the dull exterior was a solid-gold Buddha. It had been covered over centuries before during a war-time to protect it from the enemy soldiers.

We are that Buddha and our cleansing rituals are the hammer and chisel that will chip away the dirt and detritus of fear, denial, cruelty and lack to find the true gold within. The hardest part to chip through is the veneer; that takes courage, determination and discipline. After that, it's so fascinating you'll want to go on to find the jewel within.

Here are some suggestions:

♦ My favourite cleansing prayer comes from my own particular independent church.
Create in me a clean heart, O Forgiving Love, and renew a right spirit within me.
That touches the right chord for me but you need to find a cleansing prayer, affirmation or ritual that is right for you.

♦ Louise Hay, author of *You Can Heal Your Life,* teaches a good 'loosing' affirmation: 'I release all anger, I release all fear, I release all tension, I release all guilt, I release all resentment. I am open and receptive to all the good and abundance the Universe has for me now.'

♦ Comb down your aura. You just use both hands with fingers far apart to run down through your aura from the crown chakra to your feet several times. Then you fluff

47

up the aura from the bottom up with your fingers closer together but flexible. This is great fun to do with friends as they can feel it immediately.

♦ Make up an atomiser of cleansing remedies such as Rescue (or Recovery) Remedy, Willow (for resentment), Holly (for anger), Walnut (to ease negative effects of change) together with some lemon or other citrus oil. Spray your home and office regularly with a cleansing prayer— something like 'Through the blessing of Grace/Source, this room and everything in it is now blessed and cleansed and filled with light.'

♦ Imagine your psyche as a village with its own ocean harbour. Place great metal gates at the harbour mouth. Then look closely at the ships within your harbour. If there are any that are pollutants, or any that you don't like the look of, visually move them outside the harbour gates and close the gates tight behind them. Say 'not in *my* harbour.'
If the water in your harbour is not clean and clear then these ships have affected your psyche. Imagine a mountain behind the village, green and uninhabited. From its peak flies down an angelic presence with a grail full of holy water. The angel passes the grail to you to bless and pour into the harbour. You say words such as 'by this holy water my harbour place is cleansed and healed' and pour the water

48

into the harbour. It is then cleared with the negative energies and ships evaporating away. This may not happen 100% at once but if you return several times you will find that the water will clear steadily. You may also find that some of those ships creep back in. Send them away again. This meditation can be extended throughout the village and the island itself with time (see my workshop *The Quest of the Soul)* but, for these purposes, stick with the harbour. Once you are familiar with the visualisation, every time you experience a thought that you don't like or don't want just say 'not in *my* harbour' and mentally push the thought outside your gates in the open sea (also see the Spiritual Law of Denial).

For those of you who worry about the environment, this is not harming the planet; it is simply setting your boundaries. Negative thoughts, feelings and issues can only thrive if human beings give them attention.

THE HAWAIIAN CLEANSING TECHNIQUE.

There are more details of the Hawaiian cleaning technique called Ho'oponopono in my book *From Credit Crunch to Pure Prosperity* (O Books). The pure simplicity of that system of cleansing through affirming self-love is so powerful that it will transform underlying thoughts without your even knowing it. Joe Vitale's and Ihaleakala Hew Len's book *Zero Limits* (Wiley) has the most thorough description of the technique.

I went to an Ho'oponopono workshop with Dr. Hew Len in London in 2007 where he told us to 'clean, clean, clean' whenever someone raised a question or we felt uncomfortable and that, as a very simple mantra, also works.

But it's too simple for most people. I had a friend going through a serious health crisis who simply couldn't affirm the Ho'oponopono mantra 'I love you, I love you, I love you,' to herself endlessly as it just didn't feel difficult enough or complex enough. Instead she felt she had to make her already upset body jump through hoops because she believed that her path to healing had to be complex and painful.

How this simple affirmation of 'I love you, I love you, I love you,' works is that it engraves itself deeply in the psyche, erasing the old, worn out beliefs. No, it won't solve the big questions immediately but it will salve them, even on an everyday basis. So it's a short-term bandage and a long-term healing simultaneously. It's easier to do than Louise Hay's affirmation of 'I love myself' because it's less likely to get the rumbling ego-response of 'no you don't; you're rubbish.'

What it will definitely do is show you that you can change beliefs without even knowing it.

I used to dislike the part of the evening known as 'gloaming', when it's not dark and it's not light—it's dusky and grey-looking. When I was a child and more psychic than I understood I found it an eerie and frightening time and, ever since then, I have believed that I don't like the gloaming.

Almost exactly a year after I did the Ho'oponopono training with Dr Hew Len I was driving to Edinburgh with my husband and we were in the middle of the countryside when dusk fell.

'Isn't it beautiful?' I said, genuinely meaning it

and amazed at how lovely the landscape looked. My husband eyed me quizzically.

'But you don't like the gloaming,' he said.

'So I don't,' I said, perplexed as my mind tried to re-assert its old pattern. 'But you know, actually, I do!'

It took me quite a few minutes to realise that the old dislike had completely vanished. There was no other reason why it should have, except that it was an old, worn out belief replaced by love.

Since repeating Ho'oponopono for nearly two years now I've discovered that I'm quite happy with a lot of previous dislikes, varying from the music of Crosby, Stills and Nash and TRex to the colour mauve. Those may sound trivial but the energy of dislike and disapproval are really quite draining and a definite block to abundance so dropping any of them is going to help.

Be gentle with yourself but cleanse something every day if you can. Just mentally place any unhappy thought outside of your harbour gates…

ON FORGIVENESS

Holding on to anger, pain and resentment don't harm the other person or situation; they harm us. I've come across quite a few books that say 'forgive' but don't tell you *how* to forgive. The good news is that any cleansing technique—especially Ho'oponopono—will dissolve the blocks in you that are holding on to the pain.

Forgiveness can also come more easily if you are a living a happy and profitable life. So to focus on prosperity is a wonderful way to sort out old issues of hatred and anger. The singer and actress Bertice Reading told a friend of mine that the best revenge is to live a good life and she was right. If you are moving on and branching out, what *they* did to you cannot hold onto your psyche.

Quite often, not forgiving is an excuse not to try, not to move on and not to succeed. If you can blame the ever-present *them* for your failure it's a great excuse. But excuse is all it is. Remember that you need to move up the scale from depression and despair through revenge/rage, anger, frustration etc. If you are constantly angry it's because you have become trapped in a cycle of anger and depression and need to act to get your feelings out. What's most likely happening is that you feel furious and others placate you (you can't blame them; you're a fiery furnace!). You'll need to go through your anger somewhere quiet or alone (see Chapter One for tips) but go through it, you must.

SUGGESTIONS FOR THE FORGIVENESS PROCESS.

♦ Whenever the person or the situation comes up *throw* them out of your harbour! That's a brief moment of expressive anger that carries you straight from unhappiness to the possibility of hope.

♦ Express how you feel with a letter to the person who has offended you (write it and then burn it; don't send it, for goodness' sake!). Really go for it with all the blame you can muster. In most cases, you'll find yourself winding down quite naturally by allowing yourself to be totally vile for once.

♦ You can also do it by imagining them in a pink tutu and ballet shoes and tights, if they are a bloke, or in shoulder-high fishing waders with soaked hair and a trout on their head if they are a girl. Anything that makes them look ridiculous in your eyes will help. Remember the *riddikulus* spell in J. K. Rowling's *Harry Potter and the Prisoner of Azkaban* (Bloomsbury)? It changes a boggart, which is a magical creature that takes on the form of your greatest hatred or fear, into something that will make you laugh. Nothing dissolves pain or anger like laughter. If you practise this one regularly, you'll find that most situations that used to make you mad will make you laugh instead. Recently, my husband did something fairly trivial that, ten years ago, would have made me furious. It tried to be angry with him; really I did, but all the time I was trying it I could just see how totally silly I was making myself. And it wasn't as though I could genuinely believe that he'd done it to hurt me or because he didn't care. It was really quite frustrating not to be able to nag at him until that made me laugh again. And then we could both share the joke.

Soul-work is all about understanding that you attract the situations you find yourself in, whether it's through the unacknowledged low-grade misery inside that you may have learnt to tolerate or through negative thinking. You need to start believing that you deserve better and if you will find the discipline to cleanse your psyche, they— or the thoughts about them—will move away from you; they have to; it is law.

HOUSE BLESSING

More and more people are becoming aware of 'good' and 'bad' energies in homes and offices. I've had most of my homes aligned by a Feng Shui practitioner but, the last time the lady came, she made a mistake and, for a while, I arranged my healing and teaching room incorrectly. But the great blessing that came from that was that I could *feel* that the orientation of the room was unbalanced.

Once I got over the 'but she's an expert; you don't know anything' aspect, and taught myself a little basic Feng Shui, I changed the room orientation again. However, that meant that the altar area was in the West whereas my spiritual training says that it 'should' be in the East.

As you can tell, this was a huge lesson in what truly feels right as opposed to what other people say is the correct way to do it.

I went with my instinct and placed the altar where I wanted it and when my spiritual teacher came to stay a few months later he said, 'that's the spiritual East now; you've made it that way. That's fine.'

The question was, why didn't I know to start with what were the correct areas for me to work, pray and teach when I *did* know later on?

The answer is because the Feng Shui lady taught me to light candles every day and to cleanse the room (and the whole house) with light, fragrance and sound. So the house was transformed through the cleansing and was no longer cluttered with heavy energy. It and my intuition could then tell me what was right and what was not.

I've since discovered that if you bless and cleanse your self and your home (and office) on a regular basis, you don't necessarily need a Feng Shui practitioner at all. The house's residual Feng Shui (psychological level) is over-ruled by conscious (spiritual) energy. Energy in houses rises and drops according to the energies of those who live in them and blessing your home can clear negative energies *for up to three months*. It's simple, effective—and you can do it yourself.

House Blessing cleans the atmosphere of a house so that its etheric energy becomes neutral and can then be imbued with positive, healing and life-enhancing energy. Walls retain memory and there can be residual energy from the after effects of illness, of death, divorce or relationship break-up. It's also important to cleanse a new home or if you are preparing to get pregnant.

It needs to be done four times a year for full effect but once you know what to do it's quick, easy and fun.

A basic 'home blessing kit' includes:
1. Smudge Stick
2. Smudge feather (or any kind of fan)
3. Red, blue and white candles
4. Bell/chime
5. Incense and incense holder
6. Amethyst
7. Clear quartz
8. Four clear crystal shards

But don't worry if you don't have all these; improvise and do what you can. And a white candle or tea light will always do some good!

PRACTICAL STEPS.

Before you cleanse and bless your house it is best to clear pathways to the front and back doors and clear both physical clutter and emotional clutter—old letters and objects that bring thoughts of pain. Sometimes that's the biggest task of all, of course, (see *The Little Book of Prosperity* for the importance of clutter clearing).

Clean the house and mend or throw away all the broken or damaged objects you can (without driving yourself crazy). Then set aside some time when you won't be disturbed. Centre yourself by sitting quietly and peacefully and attuning to your chosen spiritual discipline.

Ask for protection and guidance.

Light a smudge stick over a saucer or pot which will catch any ash. Blow on the sage-brush to make it smoulder. Then, using the feather to waft the smoke, walk around the entire house from the front door inwards, ensuring that smoke goes to every corner, high and low as well as in the centre of each room.

While smudging, repeat in each room, as feels appropriate:

'By the Grace of God/Spirit this room is cleansed and healed of all negativity.'

Once the house has been smudged, extinguish the smudge stick by wetting it or by putting it out in earth or sand.

Then, using your bell, chime or Tibetan bowl, go around the house again, making sound in every corner and in the centre of each room. As you do, say 'By the Grace of God/Spirit, this room is filled with clarity and joy.'

When you've finished, sit quietly and assess in your mind whether there are any parts of the house which have resisted this cleansing. It will be purely intuition that tells you this. If there is anywhere, go to it and make a loud noise such as clapping hands or banging a saucepan or a drum to dissipate the energy. Then ring the bell with the blessing again and, if you have any more doubts, light an incense stick in that room.

Once all this is done, you can dedicate the house to the Divine Light. I personally wouldn't just say 'to the light' as that's a not going to guarantee the best results... Light is relative (you've head the phrase 'dim as a Toc H lamp', haven't you?) but the Divine is Absolute.

Hold the clear quartz in your hands and say 'I dedicate you to cleansing and healing of this house and the electrical energies in it' and place it near the largest electrical equipment (computer or video). It's best to have many crystals—and plants—near electrical points.

Place the amethyst with a similar blessing on a place where it can hold clear energy—your desk or on the mantelpiece. Your intuition will tell you where you want it to be.

Use the quartz shards on the down-pipes of lavatories or basins. Stick them on with Blu-Tack so that the tip of the shard is pointing *upwards*. This will diminish the effect of energy flowing out of the house when loo or sink are used.

Find what feel to you to be the focus points of the house for:

1. Spirituality (white candles)
2. Prosperity (red candles)
3. Relationships (blue candles).

Light two blue candles together with a dedication to bring or maintain love to you (and your partner) in this home. Say something like: 'these lights symbolise the love and peace of our relationship.' It's best to light them at a time when you are spending an evening together—perhaps a meal—and will not be too distracted. You can either let them burn down or put them out and use them again. If you are seeking a relationship then bless the candles as indications of the relationship that you have with the universe and your, as yet unknown, love. Have as many images and ornaments in twos as you can to help the universe get the message.

Blue candles are also good for promoting health.

Light red candles either together or separately with affirmations of prosperity. 'Wealth, abundance and joy are alive in this house; I attract prosperity with every breath and am blessed with abundant life.'

A red candle on your work desk is very effective.

SABBATH EVE

In the Jewish tradition, the Sabbath eve is a Friday night. This is appropriate for anyone who has a five-day a week occupation. See how you feel about doing the Sabbath Eve blessing below. If it's too religious, create your own. But it's a really good thing to let your home know that the time of working is over and the time of rest is here.

On the Sabbath Eve following the house blessing (the night before your day off, whether that is Friday or Saturday night), light two white candles at dusk and ask for your day of rest to be blessed.

If you want to use the traditional Sabbath Eve prayer, here it is:

Lord of the Universe, I am about to perform the sacred duty of kindling the lights in honour of the Sabbath. Even as it is written: 'And Thou shalt call the Sabbath a delight and the holy day of the Lord honourable.'

And may the effect of my fulfilling this commandment be that the stream of abundant life and heavenly blessing flow in upon me and mine. That Thou be gracious unto us and cause thy presence to dwell among us.

Father of mercy, continue thy loving kindness unto me and unto my dear ones. Make me worthy to walk in the way of the righteous before thee, loyal to thy law and clinging to good deeds. Keep Thou far from us all manner of shame, grief and care and grant that peace, light and joy ever abide in our home. For with thee is the fountain of life; in thy light do we see light. Amen.

If it is practical, let these candles burn until they go out naturally.

SIMPLE MAINTENANCE

Once a week, light incense sticks in at least one room in the house and bless the house again. Or repeat any of the prayers with candles.

Once a month, ring the bell/chimes around the house.

Once every three months, re-smudge.

You'll know when a cleansing is needed. Look upon it in the same way as you would look upon weeding your garden. If it's done, the place looks and feels good; if it's neglected then plants/energies that you prefer not to have around may over-run your chosen flowers.

EXERCISE THREE

(as if there weren't enough throughout the chapter!)

Create your own Mikvah.

Once a week have a specific cleansing and purifying bath. Make sure you have some time undisturbed where you can relax. Switch that telephone off!

Firstly, wash yourself all over from head to foot—perhaps in the shower. Then draw yourself a bath with herbal essences, aromatherapy oils or whatever scents you love to inhale.

Light candles—as many as you like but one is just fine.

Sink yourself down into the bath and relax. At some stage, duck your head and hair below the water making sure that all of you is covered.

Say some words of blessing or cleansing. Here is a lovely traditional Buddhist prayer for blessing and healing.

Just as the soft rains fill the streams, pour into the rivers, and join together in the oceans, so may the power of every moment of your goodness flow forth to awaken and heal all beings—those here now, those gone before, those yet to come.

By the power of every moment of your goodness, may our heart's wishes be soon fulfilled as completely shining as the bright full moon, as magically as by a wish-fulfilling gem.

By the power of every moment of your goodness, may all dangers be averted and all disease be gone. May no obstacle come across our way. May we enjoy fulfillment and long life.

For all in whose heart dwells respect, who follow the wisdom and compassion, of the Way, may our life prosper in the four blessings of old age, beauty, happiness and strength.

When you are ready, get out of the bath, dry yourself consciously and lovingly, appreciating your body and how well it works. Then dress in clean, pretty/elegant clothes and celebrate with a lovely meal or a drink

THE SPIRITUAL LAW OF HONESTY

'To thine own self be true; and it must follow, as the night the day, thou canst not then be false to any man.'
William Shakespeare

'Truth is one's real nature; when you are yourself, there comes a great flood of joy welling up within you; when you deny yourself and deceive yourself, shame darkens your mind and breeds fear.'
Sai Baba

'...the truth will make you free.'
Gospel of John 8:32

When was the last time you were really true to yourself?

Can you remember the time when you first started to lie?

The lies creep up on us almost un-noticed, even before our first day at school, leaving behind them a faint residue of disappointment and unease. They are very subtle and they start as soon as you agree with anyone who 'puts you in your place' or dismisses your potential.

A quick perusal of children's toy shops, TV, books and articles about 'Indigo' and 'Star' children suggests that perhaps parents nowadays don't say things like 'don't be silly,' when their offspring say, 'I'm a princess; I'm a super-hero; I want to be a writer; I am beautiful.' But most of the people who pick up this book will have been born in different days and it's in early childhood that we pick up most of our conditioning.

I wanted to be an actress when I was very young; there was nothing I enjoyed more than dressing up and putting on plays with my brother and our friends.

But I learnt to believe that an actress wasn't the kind of thing that someone from my family did. I picked up that actresses were trashy. And beautiful. And talented. And thin. I didn't want my parents to think me trashy and I knew that I wasn't beautiful (the first lie) and that I was not talented (the second lie) and that I was not thin enough (the third lie).

My mother had been a acclaimed actress and singer in amateur dramatics but gave it up when she had children (do you spot some potential for unacknowledged resentment there?). I noticed that she used to make it clear that she didn't rate female singers or actresses so I knew that such a choice of career would not be approved. Unconsciously I also believed that I must not threaten my mother's own success by outshining her.

Forty years later, to my total astonishment, my mother suddenly announced, 'You should have been an actress. You would have made a wonderful actress.'

Now my Mum has a Gemini Moon which entitles her to change her mind whenever she wants to without realising that she's even done it. And she is now a much happier woman than she was in those days. But it makes me wonder, all the same, whether she actually *would* have objected to my becoming an actress or whether it was just me lying to myself because I didn't at heart believe that I was good enough.

It was probably both but I bet you have a similar

story about something you wanted to do when you were very young.

Oh—and before we go any further, any early ambition to be in the caring services such as being a nurse or someone who looks after elderly people requires you to apply a vigorous pinch of salt. Those are *good* things to do that would have been approved by virtually anyone. They are nature's instinctive urges to make us become good parents, not the calling of our soul. Look for the inner explorer, beetle biologist, strategist, train driver or pot-holer and see what comes up for you. Wanting to be a doctor is fine; as a child it's a fascinating idea to poke people around and diagnose things! And later, if you truly want to be a nurse, that's fine too, just be sure that you are doing it from a deep sense of vocation and not because you want to be kind. Nurses in real life don't get much time to give loving kindness to their patients; they are running around fetching and carrying, administering medication, bathing and instructing their patients. That takes a lot of discipline, nerve and strength and if you talk to a professional nurse about how lovely it must be to care for others, they will most likely snort and start telling you about the problems the National Health Service.

I'm not knocking the caring services; I've been a therapist for years. But I, like many others, went into healing to salve my own pain vicariously through helping others. It's known as the Princess Diana syndrome. If there's a balance of caring for your self and inner growth together with assisting others, that's terrific but if you care, care, care without refueling yourself, you are in danger of going out of balance.

If you are in a caring profession, you will be

able to tell if you've got it right if at least *some* of the following apply to you:

♦ You have regular therapy sessions yourself—not just occasional swaps with friends.

♦ You meditate/visualise/take sacred time out for yourself at least three times a week.

♦ You don't sacrifice your own life for your clients or bosses by working all the hours of the day.

♦ You still look forward to your working day.

♦ Your clients grow and move on.

♦ You can still feel good about yourself if you don't have any clients that day/week.

♦ You don't automatically have to start taking care of your own family as soon as you get home from taking care of others all day.

♦ Your health is good—or at least getting better.

♦ You still have energy to enjoy yourself at the weekends.

♦ You take regular holidays.

♦ You buy yourself or give yourself treats on a regular basis.

♦ You can talk to a depressed client without having to drop your own energy so that you feel drained afterwards.

Through running Holistic Marketing classes I've known a lot of people who wanted to start up an holistic centre, believing that this was their goal in life and that it would be just what is needed for everyone. They want to provide a nurturing place for people to heal.

Offering yourself heart and soul as a beacon of light for the healing of others requires you to be very, very balanced and prosperous in yourself.

Many people who originally wanted to be a healer end up running a therapy centre where others can thrive, rather than having the time and energy to continue loving their own work. The initial impulse of finding one's joy in being a light for others can easily get clogged up through the organisational aspects of such a venture. If your joy isn't in administration, don't start a centre.

Organising for others when it's not your soul's work leads to a lowering of your own energy. In the case of running a therapy centre you are taking on a lot of the therapists' own financial, authority and promotion issues and are likely to face their projections on those subjects as well. As soon as working outside the sphere of your own bliss to take care of other people's administration takes up more than 50% of your time, then you are being unfaithful to yourself. This is the negative side of allowing—allowing the happiness of others to be more important than your own.

CALLING ALL REBELS!

Not all of us are programmed to be carers or 'good children.' Rebellion in order to be the focus of attention is another way that we learn not to be our true selves. The rebel is usually thought to be more of an individual and, in a way, he or she is so. However, rebels are always pushing against something rather than being in balance with themselves. They get a high from being outrageous and attracting attention that way while carers get a high from being thought kind or lovely.

It's also interesting to note that most rebels simply join a different tribe. We are all part of tribes—family, social group, work etc. It's an integral part of being a member of the animal kingdom. Many people are happy to remain tribal forever but if you are reading this book you have aspirations to be more than a tribal being. You want to be a fringe-dweller; someone who is developing as an individual and discovering your own, unique relationship with Source and the Universe. You'll often find that tribal people are uncomfortable with you; that you don't fit into any of their boxes. That's individuation rather than rebellion. The Shaman or healer is never truly a part of the tribe; he or she lives on the edge. Rebels always belong to a particular group whether it's Punk Rock, Hell's Angels, Goths or whatever. In that way they are tribally no different from people who join a particular religion or belief system.

Rebels need to get attention, even if it is negative attention, in order to prove to themselves that they are different and special. Often they need to make the normal people 'wrong' and act as if only they have the courage and spirit to step away from the stupid ones who don't understand. I remember trying to join a rebel group at school and feeling terribly superior (very briefly!) when I realised that I was in with a chance of becoming one of the current in-crowd. The trouble was, I didn't actually *like* any of them and none of them liked me. I did at least have the sense to realise that this mattered!

Spiritual people need community — people of like mind who can hold up a mirror to us and help us to develop in an environment of support, laughter and love — but our work is to develop soul-group energies rather than tribal systems. The trick is working out which spiritual systems and groups are alive and which have become tribes. One clue is that if the group needs to make any other similar group wrong, it is tribal. Ego has to prove itself to be right and tribe is run by ego-consciousness.

Even the most developed spiritual group can become lost in tribe if it starts to crystallise. I went to a group in London for sixteen years which was clear, bright and open. But in the last three years of my attendance, it seemed to me that it became more social than spiritual and the elderly leader began to pull back into the faith system of his birth. He became uncomfortable with those who openly practiced within other traditions. There also emerged 'the Usual Suspects,' a group who went to absolutely everything that was organised and who thought that this spiritual tradition was the centre of the Universe. No other aspects of it taught by different teachers, even of the same religion, need apply!

When the founder told me, on a foreign trip with the group where I had chosen to do some extra travelling instead of going to his workshop, 'We are all family here and you should show up otherwise it is disrespectful to the group,' I knew it was my cue to leave. In the days when group was still my spiritual inspiration, he would have said, 'Did you have fun? Did you learn anything?' or 'Is anything wrong that you didn't want to come?'

It's not easy to leave tribe, family, work or environment but if they are causing you to be dishonest within yourself, then it will show in your prosperity and your levels of happiness.

I wept for two full hours after I realised that my participation in this group was over as it had become very dear to me over the years. But I knew I could no longer grow and develop as an individual in that environment. And as soon as I made the decision, I got a new book contract for something close to my heart that I had previously resisted writing because I believed that my former teacher would not have approved of it.

BEING HONEST ABOUT MONEY.

Most of us hate to admit that we would like more money. It's fine to talk about prosperity and abundance because they 'mean so much more than money.' But if you can own up to wanting oodles and oodles of cash just for the fun of it, then you're opening some important doors in your psyche.

Here are some of the excuses for not being wealthy:

♦ *Justification*: If I had it, it would take it away from somebody else who needs it more.

♦ *Answer*: If someone doesn't have prosperity consciousness then they can't attract or keep prosperity. If they do, they don't need you to be poor in order to have

68

their own energy aligned. So you simply *can't* take anything away from another through your own prosperity.

That's it in a nutshell. And if you push prosperity onto someone who is not ready for it, then you are handing out abuse.

Abuse? Yes, actual abuse. You'll have heard those stories about kids given Porsches when they were 17 years old and wrapping them around lamp posts. You've seen those stories on the news about youngsters killing themselves by crazy driving on a night out. If you give people something they are not up to vibration with, then they will use it to harm themselves or it will lead to someone else harming them.

Many years ago I was on a train from Cusco to Lake Titicaca in Peru. We were advised to keep the carriage doors locked (which was tricky as the loo was in a separate place between carriages) and also to padlock our suitcases to the overhead luggage racks. This was because of the kids who would swarm all over the train to try and beg—and steal—from the tourists.

At every stop, the train was besieged by youthful beggars and at one place I saw an elderly lady who was keeping a safe distance at the end of the station, behind all the supple young boys but who also was begging. I thought I would try and help her so I waited until the train was moving away and then threw her a book, which she could have sold.

Her face lit up as the book landed at her feet—and then five boys leapt on her, threw her to the ground and fought over the book. They left her unconscious, maybe even dead as they ran off with the prize.

Had I helped that old woman? No. My intentions

were good but not understanding the pack-animal ferocity of the youths, I had been the instrument of causing her pain.

Another time, when I worked in London, I used to pass a beggar on the street every night on the way to the Tube. He was a pleasant enough fellow and I often gave him a pound or so. One day, when I'd received a bonus, I gave him a twenty pound note. The next evening I found him drunk, covered in bruises and, lying in a doorway surrounded by broken glass.

Now, it was this man's choice what he did with that £20 but he was in no fit vibrational state to make a sensible decision. It wasn't actually my responsibility and it is, of course, possible that he woke up the next day, went to a hostel and joined Alcoholics Anonymous. But even so, I didn't feel good about my part in the situation.

What I'm trying to get at here is that if we over-help people it will rebound on them and on us. It's a very fine balance as we all want to be generous in our hearts. However, you may have noticed that for all the charity auctions, telethons, fund-raisers, jumble-sales, collections, promotions, bags-through-the-door and shops, there seems to be no less demand for us to help. I would suggest that this is because the people who need the help are not being taught prosperity consciousness. If they don't have the vibrational level to be at peace with the money coming to them, it cannot do them any lasting good.

Millions and millions and millions of money has been raised for charity over the last 20 years or so (look at Band Aid/Live Aid) but there is no slackening of the appeals for more and more and more. *If charity were working, we would be solving the problems*. It's not money that's needed; it's consciousness.

♦ *Justification*: There isn't enough to go round.

♦ *Answer*: There is enough printed money on this planet for every single inhabitant to be a millionaire. *And* only two per cent of the money in the world is even printed. The rest is 'understood to exist' i.e. it's imaginary.

There is no lack of money—even in times of what the corporate world and the media call a recession. It's just a question of the distribution. And as money is energy it responds to our corresponding energy. If we are afraid of lack then we project a low energy on financial matters. Money is an invention of human beings in order to make exchange easy and fair. It may well be that some people abuse the energy but we don't have to be a part of that and we don't have to give it unnecessary attention.

If all the printed money in the world were to be distributed equally to every living person, it's most likely that, in five years' time, it would be back where it is right now. That's because it is drawn to those who vibrate with wealth and prosperity and it can't stay with those who vibrate with lack. That's the Law of Attraction, pure and simple. It's not nice but it doesn't have to be. That's not its job.

♦ *Justification*: Being wealthy is selfish and spiritually wrong.

♦ *Answer*: This is old religious and

71

social training from people who don't understand the ancient texts or why they were written.

Religious and spiritual attitudes to money form a large part of my books *The Little Book of Prosperity, From Credit Crunch to Pure Prosperity* and my CD *Pure Prosperity*. However, it is one of the noted dichotomies of the world that the Christian Church has often taught that it is appropriate to be spiritual and poor and yet has built the most beautiful and expensive churches in honour of God. And the Vatican, of course, is one of the wealthiest places in the world.

If we are children of the Source then we are automatically worthy whatever we do. If you are not wealthy then you can't do much to help other people become wealthy; it truly would be the blind leading the blind.

In other times when we weren't able to research and study different faiths for ourselves, such attitudes were understandable but nowadays, with interfaith options, the Internet and holistic teachings, we can see that the great spiritual teachers never lacked for anything and that many of the people lauded as saints were, at least, not living lives that would be appropriate today and, at worst, ego-bound in the search for martyrdom. Take St. Rose of Lima for example: from the age of 20, she wore a metal spiked crown, concealed by roses, and an iron chain about her waist. She would fast for days, taking just a drink of bitter herbs. When she could no longer stand, she sought repose on a bed constructed by herself, of broken glass, stone, potsherds and thorns. She died fourteen years later from self-neglect. That's not holy; it's a denial of both God's goodness and of life itself. Today, Rose would be considered anorexic and seriously in need of help.

Every spiritual tradition must update for the times in which we live. To hold ancient beliefs in the form they were in times gone by is to kill a living tradition.

It is still true that—as said earlier—possessions can possess us rather than the other way round. But true prosperity is about abundant energy and abundant joy. You can experience those in a field looking at flowers or in purchasing a Luis Vuitton bag. Whatever does it for you, you have my blessing (should you even *consider* needing it!). It's about being true to *you*, not about being true to trained-in beliefs.

♦ Justification: Wealth corrupts.

♦ Answer: So does poverty; so does power—*if* we let them.

Yes, there are wealthy people in the world who do terrible things, both consciously and unconsciously. But so do people who haven't enough to eat; so do people who are addicted to drugs; so do people who don't understand each individual's right to believe according to their conscience.

Wealth, money, prosperity etc. can all be summed up by *feeling*. You may have everything that everyone else in the world considers to be wealth but if you are unhappy then you have nothing. And it is those who are unhappy who cause the harm in this world.

The quotation from the Gospel of Mark (8:36), '*For what shall it profit a man, if he shall gain the*

73

whole world, and lose his own soul?' doesn't mean that you can't or shouldn't be wealthy; it means that striving after wealth in a way that causes you to be dishonest about your self will destroy you. It's the compromises that we make in order to get people to like us; buy from us; agree with us that hurt our true selves. And it is perfectly possible to be prosperous by being your true self.

How do you do that? You spend 50% or more of your day focusing on finding the better, more prosperous thought. It doesn't have to be a big thought or a hugely wealthy thought—you don't have to fantasise about winning the lottery (although if that makes you feel good, then do it!). All most people want in their financial life is a comma in their bank account. Because where there's a comma, three noughts will automatically follow. So when you look at your bank account, put a mental comma after the figure and see the three noughts materialise.

This will not corrupt you. It may please you or amuse you but if it does neither, then don't do it! As long as you are feeling good then you are prosperous.

EXERCISE FOUR:

Journal your feelings every half-hour for a week. It doesn't have to be an epic; just note down event, conversation, feeling anytime something happens. Then you can see exactly what lifts your energy and exactly what drops it. The lifting of energy comes from being in alignment with yourself and the Source. The dropping of energy means moving away from your true self. Noticing it brings it to the conscious level instead of letting it drone away beneath.

Some of this dropping of levels may come when

someone interrupts you while you are doing what you want to do—that's quite natural. But some of it will be habitual on seeing or talking to someone or on certain tasks that you have to do.

'But I have to do them; it's my work!' you can answer. Yes, but are you on the right bus?

Ken Robert runs a blog on www.mildlycreative. com. He's the first to say he's not an expert on anything in particular but his article '*Are you on the wrong bus?*' will tell you whether you're being honest with yourself. If you are on the wrong bus—whether it's at work, in a relationship or lifestyle—*you will be going in the wrong direction*. And if you are going in the wrong direction for you then you will surely end up somewhere where you don't want to go.

Ken has kindly let me quote his article and I strongly recommend you sign up for his free inspiration email and newsletter.

You can tell you're on the wrong bus if:

1. You bought your ticket using price as your sole criterion.

If money's the only thing keeping you at your job, that's a very strong sign you're on the wrong bus. You wouldn't take a bus to Birmingham when you want a trip to Edinburgh because a Birmingham ticket was half the cost, would you? Why are you settling for work that sucks the life out of you, even for higher pay, when you deeply desire to be inspired and energised? Drudgery at double the salary is still drudgery.

2. You caught the first bus out of town.

Did you take your current job because it was the first you could get? Maybe your circumstances didn't allow you to be choosey, but that was yesterday. Start taking steps right now to change buses (better job) or get your own car (self-employment).

3. You took this bus because everyone else was taking it.

Your parents did this work; maybe your family has been doing it for generations. But you're all grown up now and life is not a game of *Simon Says*. Start exploring other destinations, find out where you want to go, and look for the first safe exit. If your parents had been axe murderers would you have followed their example?

4. You find yourself looking out the window and wondering all the time...

That bus you're on, the job you took some time ago, might well have been just the thing you needed then. You may have learnt the ins and outs of a business, developed skills you never knew you had and paid the bills, but maybe it's still time to change. It's okay to grow. Change that wondering to a real daydream and find out where you want to go next.

5. You just can't wait until the stupid thing stops.

Constantly checking your watch is perhaps the number one sign you're on the wrong bus. If you're bored you'll watch the clock. But if you're taking the steps to build your own vision rooted in things you truly love and serving the kind of people you love, you'll only check your watch to make sure you haven't missed an entire day.

THE SPIRITUAL LAW BEHIND THE TEN COMMANDMENTS.

If men will not be governed by the Ten Commandments, they shall be governed by the ten thousand commandments.
G.K. Chesterton

The Ten Commandments aren't prefaced with 'if you're in the mood.'
Dr. Laura Schlesinger

My own spiritual tradition is based on the metaphysics behind the Bible. I fully acknowledge the validity of other faiths and I've been inspired by many modern teachers of prosperity and spirituality but my soul's journey is to make sense of the tradition into which I was born. If you were born into a nominally Christian society, there will be echoes of Biblical lore in your psyche, so it's a good idea to understand the original intentions behind them in case they are causing prosperity problems.

That means going back to the roots — back to the original ten laws that formed the basis of Judaism, Christianity and Islam: The Ten Commandments.

At first sight, the commandments look rather demanding, and even mean, but my years in Jewish mystical circles have taught me the metaphysical meanings behind them and now they make good sense to me as a prosperity student and teacher.

The commandments give clear guidelines for prosperous living, no matter what day and age you live in, and they are all practical examples of how the Law of Attraction works.

We are told in the Torah (the first five books of the Old Testament of the Bible) that the commandments were given twice; the first time, verbally, in Exodus 20 and the second, written in stone, in Exodus 32. This was to demonstrate that the commandments have inner (esoteric) and outer (exoteric) meanings. Just as many of our nursery rhymes and children's stories have hidden meanings behind the obvious story.

The first three commandments are the most important—and the most misunderstood.

THE FIRST COMMANDMENT

I am the LORD thy God, which have brought thee out of the land of Egypt, out of the house of bondage. Thou shalt have no other gods before me.

Please note that it doesn't say that there *are* no other gods; there were—and are—many. In Biblical days there were dozens of gods—Greek, Roman, Pagan, gods of the home, of work, of prosperity, of war, of love of nature. Even though the Israelites believed in the ultimate God, even that one God had many different names and levels—aspects of the Divine. And the gods of other people might have been anathema to the Israelites themselves but they figured largely in the life of people around them and other people's beliefs certainly impinged on the Jewish people's lives. In the story of Jacob and Rachel in Genesis, Rachel steals her father Laban's idols and uses mandrakes for magic because she was so desperate to have a baby. Women in Jesus' time were known to use models of the fertility god Bes to promote safe childbirth.

People are people and if a useful-looking god turns up when we need help, we will give it a go.

You only have to look at the multitudes of books about angels nowadays to see how we have updated this tradition; the angels are to us what the gods were in ancient days. They make us feel good because we understand their benevolent nature and we need to use systems and gods/spiritual beings that resonate with us to work well with the Law of Attraction. Angels carry our messages and prayers to the Source, so they are a safe and loving alternative to dealing with the Big Boss directly. But they are not to be worshipped; they are assistants on our spiritual path.

The modern esoteric meaning of this commandment, however, is wider: it means that if we do not put our own, individual relationship with Divinity first in our life then we cannot prosper. That is because the Source is just that: the source of all goodness. *Everything* comes from the Source whether it comes via work, family or the lottery.

A god is not necessarily a mythical entity worshipped in a temple; it is anything that rules you to the extent that you do not question it. Nowadays, without realising it, we regard matters such as celebrity, sex, football, money, work, drugs, victimhood, social convention and television as our gods. Putting these lesser gods before our relationship with the Source means that Grace cannot be received and life becomes a repetitive cycle of fear or the search for excitement—the highs and lows that ultimately lead to disillusionment.

Money is definitely a god. In *The Little Book of Prosperity* I looked at St. Paul's teaching on money — the well-known phrase 'the love of money is the root of all evil.' The Greek word translated for 'love of money' means 'avarice' and avarice means obsession with money, whether you have it or you don't. I know from nasty personal experience that when you are broke and in debt you are obsessed with money and how you are going to pay the next round of bills. That is one of two negative sides of the love of money (the other being the obsession with making more and more and more when you already have sufficient). St. Paul's teaching is a warning not to lose your soul in the worship of an energy form that cannot do anything but respond to the Law of Attraction. If you feel fear and dread over financial matters, then it will bring you more cause to feel both those emotions. You give money power to hurt you and, by Karmic Law, it must.

Incidentally, the word generally translated as 'evil' is *kaka* which is a slang word for excrement... so, if you'll forgive my language, it's just as accurate to say 'obsessing over money is the source of all shit in your life.'

By the Law of First Attention, it is important to put your spiritual purpose and relationship with the Source of all abundance first in all matters. The mention of Egypt in the first commandment is a reference to the Exodus from Egypt when the Israelites were released from slavery. The worship of money is slavery because it binds you and pulls you and dictates how your life feels and works. When I was in serious financial trouble I would have to check my bank accounts daily in order to juggle overdrafts. That ruled the day — slavery.

Having a relationship with the Divine does

not mean going to Church, Mosque, Temple or Synagogue; it means dropping the pre-conceived, second-hand interpretations of Divinity that we learned as children and making peace with the idea of a creative force for Good. This force can take you out of slavery if you put your attention onto it rather than onto the problems.

THE SECOND COMMANDMENT

Thou shalt not make unto thee any graven image, or any likeness of any thing that is in heaven above, or that is in the earth beneath, or that is in the water under the earth: Thou shalt not bow down thyself to them, nor serve them: for I the Lord thy God am a jealous God, visiting the iniquity of the fathers upon the children unto the third and fourth [generation] of them that hate me; And shewing mercy unto thousands of them that love me, and keep my commandments.

No graven image. Hmmm. Christianity blew that one in a big way, didn't it? There are images of God throughout Christendom. And as Christianity teaches that Christ is God, all the crucifixes in Church, around people's necks and on altars must also be violations of this second commandment. Not to mention the ceiling of the Sistine Chapel...

Why would there be a commandment for no images? Because an image can make something seem finite, allowing no personal interpretation; no argument. It is because of Christianity's misunderstanding of this commandment that so many people see God as the old man in the sky. The whole idea of the One God is meant to be that It is sexless, formless, absolute — not human male, not human female, not white nor black, not old nor young and not limited to any one religion either.

Islam and orthodox Judaism take this commandment very seriously—there are no images in synagogues or mosques. The Hindu faith appears to do the opposite—it has so many gods representing so many aspects of divinity with so many images that the devout can choose the one with which they are comfortable. This is the issue at point. In fact, Hinduism is *not* pantheistic; all the gods and goddesses are representations of Vishnu/God—different aspects of that same Source energy. It can be very helpful to focus on one particular god/energy for a particular project or issue but it needs to be remembered that there is a greater Source that understands *all* aspects of our life—and can see the wider picture. You could be seriously out of balance if you only focused on one god. A good example would be praying or invoking to Kamadiva (the Hindu equivalent of Cupid) for a certain person to love you when the whole of Source knows that person could only bring you pain. There is great subtlety in this as calling on the energy of Kamadiva to bring love and passion into your life is fine. That's because you are aligning yourself to the energy of Source through this aspect and you are willing to let It assist you in the way that is for your greatest good and happiness.

The multitude of images in Hinduism are representations of the hugeness of Source. The idea is that we see so many aspects in them that we don't focus down on just one and make it God.

The Japanese faith of Shinto has many *Kamis* or local gods, all of which contribute to the Spirit of Kami and the Ultimate Kami. We too are destined to be Kami (just as the Western Esoteric tradition talks of the Christ within). No specific images of ultimate Kami exist however.

Mystically, the commandment is *not* about having no pictures of divinity or of anything on the earth or the water under the earth. It means don't set up the precedent of how they *have* to be, look or act.

Is there anyone reading this who never read a magazine as a teenager and felt inadequate when faced with the images of perfect man or womanhood within it? That's the graven image to which the commandment refers. The 'perfect' Western woman, for example, is a supermodel: young, 5'8" tall, slender to the point of skinniness, usually blonde and with perfect, tanned skin. Anything other than that, it is hinted, is undesirable. Fewer than two per cent of Western women actually look that way but people in the 21st century frequently resort to chemicals and surgery to get closer to this graven image of the ideal.

Occasionally, we rise up against the fashion— especially when female models at size zero are promoted as a good thing—but mostly we attempt to follow the mode of the day, whether it flatters us or not.

My husband and I recently had a photo-shoot for publicity purposes and the lovely, young female photographer blanked out all my facial lines in the images that she prepared for us. Gone was everything that marked the experiences of 53 years that made me what I am. I looked lovely—like a 25-year-old—but I didn't look real and I wasn't willing to use any of those pictures.

Another example would be pedigree dogs some of which are so highly-bred that they have serious

physical flaws. If your pedigree dog has ears that
are too short or a nose that is too thin, it's not
acceptable within the breed standard. No matter
that it's a brilliant dog and a great companion.
We've had two Beagles; the second one, Puzzle,
is a former show bitch whose granddaughter won
Best of Breed at Crufts. She is utterly beautiful
and perfect according to the Kennel Club; a real
example of what a Beagle 'should' be. She's also
adorable, loving and delightful but as a hound
she's a disaster! She is totally unco-ordinated and
has no idea how to connect a scent with a potential
prey, even though Beagles are meant to be hunting
dogs. On one of her walks, she was knocked over
by a rabbit that she accidentally surprised in the
undergrowth. Both creatures got up, slightly dazed,
and ran in opposite directions. Luckily for us,
Puzzle is healthy and happy but she is gloriously
dim. She was called Puzzle before we got her and
it is more of a description than a name.

Our previous Beagle, Didcot, was too chunky,
her nose was too thin and her tail too raggedy.
Her legs were too short and her colouring was
imperfect. The Kennel Club didn't think anything
of her at all. But what a hound! Didcot was a hunter
and all dog. She was also loyal, sassy and cute and
she knew her own worth. When I came back to the
UK from Montana, USA, I had to take Didcot to
Spain and find care for her for six months so she
could come home on Passports for Pets (in those
days, you couldn't go straight from the US to the
UK). That meant leaving her on a hill farm with a
lovely family who cared for her. Didcot adapted;
she went hunting with the other dogs on the farm;
annexed the best chair by the fire and, one day
when they were late home, put herself to bed in the

hen house where it was good and warm instead of sitting outside the door waiting to be let in.

UNITY AND DUALITY

The 'no graven image' commandment does not mean that we should not strive for excellence; just that we should guard against making one image the *only* right image.

Even more importantly, a graven image of God makes Source an external thing. If you can see God then you can believe that you are separate from God. If you are separate from God you believe in duality, which is a short step from believing that your beliefs are right and other people with different beliefs are wrong; that your religion is the only path to God and that all those who don't believe what you do must be converted, ridiculed or destroyed.

We all look different and think differently. There is one Source Energy but if there are six billion people in the world, there must be six billion paths to that God. They are all valid.

The jealous God aspect of the second commandment also causes some problems in interpretation: it is usually thought to be a reference to the traditional mean and nasty Old Testament God, the one that blasts cities, demands that Philistines have their foreskins cut off and floods the world because we have made him feel rather irritated.

In his book *Prosperity* Charles Fillmore, the founder of Unity Church, explains that the Hebrew word used for 'jealous' — *kannaw* — means 'jealous of principle.' This principle, Charles explains, is the Law of Attraction. So this is an injunction that if we make our graven images and stand by them, then they are what we will receive in return. The *Baghavad Gita* puts this well: 'As you worship me, so shall you come to me.'

Interestingly, the word 'generation' does not exist in the original Hebrew of this commandment and has been added in translation, apparently for clarity. Mystics believe that the sentence refers instead to third and fourth incarnations, meaning that the soul returns to Earth to receive in future lives what it gave out in earlier ones, whether good or bad.

So this commandment is entirely about the Law of Attraction—that what we focus our attention on we will experience, in this life or another. Believe in an angry God and that belief comes back to you; believe in a world of lack and lack is reflected back to you. This takes us straight back to the first commandment; put anything before Source—ultimate Good—and that is what we will receive in return.

There is a great deal of resistance over the idea of reincarnation in the modern Christian world, even though the concept was quite acceptable to those living in Jesus' time. The possibility of multiple lives is even mentioned in the Gospels, when the disciples tell Jesus that some people think he is Elijah come again or John the Baptist reborn and also in the story of the blind man (John 9:2) where the disciples ask Jesus 'Who did sin, this man or his parents that he was born blind?'

However, the Law of Attraction is beginning to be understood again in the same manner as thousands of years ago as meaning 'like is drawn unto like.' Certainly this could mean that a murderer would be drawn to a situation where he or she might face murder but it equally means that someone who is feeling fearful will attract situations to cause more fear. This does not require a belief in reincarnation.

Those who suffered in the Spanish Inquisition or the Holocaust, for example, were affected because of the rising tide of persecution and terror which caught them up in its folds and caused them to feel severe negative emotion. This attracted more of the same and amplified it. It wasn't the Jewish people's fault; it was a normal reaction to cruelty although, of course, there must have been some aspect at the tribal level that began the focus of hostility against them. Interestingly the Jewish nation have always been the world's bankers and comfortable with dealing with finances. It's entirely possible that much of the hostility projected at them from the Inquisition may have been due to Christianity's issues with money.

Apathy or paralysis also played a part in both tragedies, in that those who could have helped may not have done so—the Christian Church, for example, did not protest at the treatment of Jews and others in the Holocaust. Those who were caught up in the tragedies also would or could not move out of the way of the threat when it first arose, due to family ties, the wish to remain in their home country or financial issues.

It is important to remember that the Karmic Law of Attraction works for good as well as bad. Every happy thought draws more happiness and every good act draws more kindness. Those who learn how to apply it consciously can face up to any situation with equanimity or even joy as in the old proverb: 'two men looked through the prison bars. One saw mud and the other saw stars.' There are many stories of heroism and amazing transformation in times of great grief or tragedy. Facing up to a situation with peace in our heart is the same as dying to the problem—just letting go of all the resistance.

We should certainly mark the great tragedies of the world, including the Holocaust and the Inquisition, but we should not wallow in them and make them an excuse to attract more persecution. We need to seek the good and move forward instead.

THE THIRD COMMANDMENT.

Thou shalt not take the name of the Lord thy God in vain; for the Lord will not hold him guiltless that taketh his name in vain.

What is the name of God?

In this quotation, it is *Yahweh Elohim,* translated by Jewish mystics as 'The Holy One', a generic description of Source Energy. However, this commandment refers back to the ultimate name of God as given to Moses in Exodus 3.13-15.

And Moses said unto God, Behold, when I come unto the children of Israel, and shall say unto them, The God of your fathers hath sent me unto you; and they shall say to me, What is his name? what shall I say unto them?

And God said unto Moses, I AM THAT I AM: and he said, Thus shalt thou say unto the children of Israel, I AM hath sent me unto you.

And God said moreover unto Moses, Thus shalt thou say unto the children of Israel, The Lord God of your fathers, the God of Abraham, the God of Isaac, and the God of Jacob, hath sent me unto you: this is my name for ever, and this is my memorial unto all generations.

The name of God is *I Am that I Am*. For the mystic this refers to God the Transcendent, the Absolute All, and God the Immanent, the part within us that is also God. We are Source Energy. As children of Source we are creative partners with Source.

So to take the name of God in vain is not to say, 'Oh my God!' but to misuse the phrase 'I Am.'

To say 'I am stupid; I am unworthy; I am no good; I am hopeless,' is to take the name of God in vain, as is to make a promise as in 'I am going to call my mother' and not doing it. You are a spark of divinity incarnate; your every word is a command to the Universe so it is wise to use the Name wisely!

The Jews were/are not allowed to say the name of God. This was probably because of its power and the possibility of misusing the I AM to bring terrible consequences but there is another likely reason. God has ten names which are spread throughout the Old Testament.

Each one of them is a different aspect of divinity, so to call on one of them is to invoke a divine attribute. Universal Law is paramount; even God doesn't break it. So if one of God's children calls on one aspect on divinity, then that aspect must be the one that answers.

As we've already seen, meditation on a name of God is not taking it in vain, rather it is aligning one's self with Source.

In Midrash, Halakkah, Talmud and the mystical teaching of Bible times, God is said to have ten aspects (one for each of the Ten Commandments). They are:

♦ **Eheyeh Asher Eheyeh** — I Am That I Am

♦ **Yahweh** – the Wisdom of God (usually translated as **Jehovah**)

♦ **Elohim** — the Knowledge or Understanding of God

♦ **El** — the Mercy of God

♦ **Yah** — the Judgment of God

♦ **Yahweh Elohim** — the Holy One or The Creator

♦ **Yahweh Zevaot** — the Hosts of Yahweh

♦ **Elohim Zevaot** — The Hosts of Elohim

♦ **El Hai Shaddai** — The Living Almighty

♦ **Adonai** — Lord. (The doorkeeper/ superintendent of household or husband). Adonai is also known as the place of the Messiah and as Shekhinah, the Daughter of the Voice.

If a Jew were to use a name for God it would be Yahweh, the Wisdom of God.

The rest of the ten commandments are simpler to understand but also have a slightly wider esoteric meaning than we have come to understand.

THE FOURTH COMMANDMENT

Remember the Sabbath and keep it holy.

This is certainly an injunction to rest, relax and take a day off once in a week but not in such a way that we are bored, restless or restricted. Constant influxes of stressful energy not only harm us but they also lead to 'sick building syndrome'. Buildings need rest, too, so that all the busy atmosphere in them can die down and dissolve. It is about taking a time of separation from the daily round where we forget our divinity all too easily.

This is intended to be a time of joy, relaxation and release and, in a world of workaholism, is more than relevant. In the modern world it could just as much mean 'turn the computer off for just one day a week.'

For the prosperity student, learning to take time out and relax is vital. Most of the time we are asking, asking, asking and doing, doing, doing. The Sabbath is about allowing—taking a step back and having fun so that what we have asked for can manifest without our interference. Allowing is always the hardest part. 'What, let go and trust God instead of pushing more? Oooh, I can't do *that!*'

Oh yes you can.

Relating this to the Law of Attraction is simple; to take time out for relaxation will attract even more time for relaxation and fun.

THE FIFTH COMMANDMENT

Honour thy father and mother

This is an injunction to remember both the sacred masculine and feminine and also to honour the tradition of your birth. We were all born into a specific time and belief system and our task is to make peace with that, even if we don't wish to embrace it.

It does refer to our own parents too. It doesn't mean that we have to like them, or even love them, but that we will be happier if we understand where they come from and how they were raised. Many an emotionally-battered child has been able to accept, if not forgive, his or her parents when he or she has been realised how unkindly they were raised themselves.

To paraphrase Oprah Winfrey, we need to forgive but that doesn't mean we have to eat chicken salad with them. If you don't want see your parents, that's your choice but try to perceive why they are how they are.

In mystical terms, 'father' means active and 'mother' means receptive so it is advice to balance ourselves between the two pillars of being. If we give too much we often forget to receive—and to refuse to receive is to deny others the joy of giving. That is the ultimate selfishness!

In terms of the Law of Attraction this is about making peace with what is, rather than resisting it. If we can see different sides of the story we can cease fighting what is. If we don't like what is and put negative attention on it, it just gets bigger. If we can find a place of acknowledgement or understanding then we can focus our attention elsewhere, towards the good.

THE SIXTH COMMANDMENT

Do not commit murder

The commandment is *not* 'do not kill.' That is a mistranslation dating back to St Jerome in the fourth century CE. There is no commandment not to kill another human; it is never advisable but sometimes it is unavoidable. If you were in such a low vibrational space that someone attacked you or your child you would hit out in return and maybe that would kill the other. But that would only happen if you were already steeped in negativity.

Murder, on the other hand, is a premeditated act carried out consciously. Esoterically it includes destroying someone's emotional or spiritual life as well as their physical life. It is murder to belittle someone's good ideas or hopeful thoughts. We do it to ourselves as well, destroying our spiritual life by living in a way that is self-destructive. The student of the Law of Attraction will understand that you would only destroy something in anyone else's life if you were deeply out of balance in your own and such bitterness, fury or rage could only bring equivalent destruction into your own life.

THE SEVENTH COMMANDMENT

Do not commit adultery.

This means not mixing together two things which harm each other or simply can't relate to each other. Marital infidelity is included but, in the esoteric view, it would be seen to be equally adulterous if two people were to remain in a destructive relationship where they were damaging each other mentally and spiritually. So, many a marriage that is kept on 'for the sake of the children' is adulterous.

This could even be tantamount to emotional murder if it stops one or both of the partners from fulfilling his or her dreams or destiny.

Jesus of Nazareth coined the words, 'those

whom God has joined together let no man put asunder.' this is often taken to mean that marriages should be for life but it is not so. Many, if not most, marriages are undertaken for social, loving and sexual reasons, but not for mutual service to the Divine so they are *not* marriages where God joined the couple together. And I know from personal experience that, if a marriage that was dedicated to Source has become spiritually adulterous, God is perfectly capable of breaking it up!

In prosperity terms, it is adulterous to speak of lack when your desire is to be prosperous or to criticise those who have what you aspire to have. Sometimes it is adulterous to go home to your family at Christmas if you find that doing so will throw you so much out of balance that you feel uncomfortable and under attack for your beliefs. We're back to tribe again — so often we feel that we 'should' spend time with people who bring down our energy. The secret is not to cut them off completely but to work on ourselves more so that we can be comfortable whatever their views. That way they have to change or move away themselves.

THE EIGHTH COMMANDMENT

Do not steal.

This includes theft of ideas or reputation or taking up so much of someone else's attention that they have no energy or time left for themselves. Although we are all responsible for how we feel and how we act, that responsibility only kicks in once we can step out of our ego. Below the threshold of consciousness we *react* rather than acting purposefully. People who are living consciously won't steal because they will realise that they are experiencing a feeling of lack within themselves even to be tempted to take something that belongs to someone else — including time. The act of theft will not solve that feeling.

Incidentally, it is not stealing if you take something without realising that it is not yours to take or if it is something like a coin dropped in the gutter. The most you can be then is the agent of the other person's Karma. If they have been careless it is the Law of Attraction rebounding on them for their own inner discomfort.

Conversely, you can steal someone's life by too much kindness. If you do everything for them to the extent that they become helpless, they cannot develop or expand their own life. Yes, of course, they are responsible for who they become but paralysis can be taught every early and it's a hard one to break out of if your every need is met.

THE NINTH COMMANDMENT

Thou shalt not bear false witness.

This refers to the giving of information that destroys good opinion — or which builds an inaccurate high opinion of someone or something. Marketing ploys are often false witness, as is second-hand gossip or any kind of hearsay.

We are exposed to a lot of false witness in the modern world with make-up advertisements advertising anti-wrinkle cream on famous faces filled with Botox and maybe even youthened by surgery.

We are also led to believe by the News that more

of the world is in trouble than is actually the case and that we should have *this* test and take *that* supplement in order to be healthy or live longer. No one believes all of it but we are all susceptible here and there.

It's also false witness to extol the virtues of a particular person, spiritual teaching or occupation if it has run its course. Most people in spiritual work know of holistic teachers who become so interested in keeping their position as the guru that they forget to do their job as teacher. Their closest students will make dozens of excuses for them, citing ill-health, business concerns, family matters and blaming those who are concerned.

It's often easier to fall into a co-dependent relationship with a finished teacher (which is also a form of adultery) than continuing our own spiritual development.

THE TENTH COMMANDMENT

Do not covet.

This is advice to appreciate what you have so that it can increase. To focus on someone else's good luck creates resentment which brings feelings of lack and unhappiness. It doesn't mean that we can't admire what others have; rather that we should focus on creating our own good instead of wasting energy destructively. It's a classic demonstration of the Law of Attraction in that it reminds us that feeling lack can only bring lack.

It's also important to realise that if you were up to speed with your own desires, then you would already have the equivalent good. And that the other person's good is very unlikely to be perfect for you. We can get very bound up in the illusion of something we think we would like rather than working out what we actually do want.

Many young people nowadays want fame because of the celebrity culture. They covet the idea of being recognised, applauded, wealthy and endorsing products in return for freebies.

I was once very famous in just one small town (I was the breakfast DJ for the very successful local radio station). That taught me the up and down sides of fame very quickly. I couldn't even buy food without comment from the store assistant; my face and figure were always under scrutiny; everything I said was either lauded or complained over and, at one stage, I attracted a stalker. I don't think he meant any harm—and God knows why he thought I wanted all that underwear—but it was terrifying to know someone was following and observing me. It led to the police putting a guard on me for a short time and that was not a pleasant experience.

Of course, I attracted it all—and to start with, it was fun and *seemed* to make up for my lack of self-esteem. But in the end, as it had to, it made me feel even worse about myself. I walked away still relatively intact but it made me very aware of the validity of the proverb 'Be careful what you ask for; you may get it.'

Of all these laws, the most important thing to remember is that the Jewish nation argued interpretations of them—and still do. Nothing is set in stone; nothing is a graven image. They were intended to protect us not to control or to frighten us and we can still use them now as reminders to live a happy and prosperous life.

EXERCISE FIVE

Check through these ten commandments to see if it is actually possible to break any one of them without the repercussions and consequences breaking all other nine. It all comes down to YOU and SOURCE.

THE SPIRITUAL LAWS OF
GIVING AND RECEIVING

'Think of giving not as a duty but as a privilege'.
John D. Rockefeller.

*'We wish to be self-sustained. We do not quite
forgive a giver. The hand that feeds us is in some
danger of being bitten'.*
Ralph Waldo Emerson

There are two types of people who are seeking
prosperity: those who give too much and those
who don't give enough.

Most of the spiritual stuff encouraging people
to give is for those who don't think about others
and don't offer help or any kind of encouragement
through their own innate fear or lack. Encouraging
someone who doesn't give is wonderful because
it will open them up. However, if you are reading
this book it's most likely that you will be on the
other end of the scale; you give and give and
give. But somehow, it doesn't seem to come back.
Something is out of balance.

Balance is vital when it comes to generosity.
And generosity is the appropriate word here
because it is just as generous to receive as it is to
give and it's important to maintain equilibrium
between the two. Quite often we don't *want* to
receive something that someone else has to offer.
If it's something that will clearly harm us then we

are correct. But if it is just a kindly gesture on their behalf and will do us no harm, to refuse it may be an act of great unkindness. Many of us have given a genuine compliment to another person only to hear them reject it. Whole conversations of irritation and accusation have been known to result from who should be allowed to be give and who should be forced to receive a compliment! My Mum was brilliant on that one; she always told me to say 'thank you' and nothing else if someone gave me a compliment. My insecure little self said 'But what if they don't mean it?' and she replied, 'then you make them look the fool.'

The very fact that I could assume that people would not give me a genuine compliment shows how much lack of self-esteem I had in those days and how I was subconsciously rejecting my good all the time. So if you can't receive a compliment, then sure as anything else, you can't receive the abundance of the Universe either, even if it is bending over backwards to offer it to you.

You can do all the visualisations and meditations you like and all the affirmations that make you feel great but if, at the end of it all, you won't receive, the Universe is stumped.

The best-known quotation on giving comes from the book of Acts in the Bible: *It is more blessed to give than to receive*. (20.35). That *seems* pretty clear. But hang on a minute and we'll look at the Biblical translation. *Makarios* is the Greek word translated as 'blessed' and it has another equally valid meaning: 'happy.'

So you could easily translate this as 'it is happier to give than to receive.' If you're a generous person that is certainly true. It's certainly a lot easier for most of us.

Here's one of my favourite quotations about giving and receiving from John Welwood, author of *Journey of the Heart* (Harper Collins):

'There is a secret about human love that is commonly overlooked: Receiving it is much more scary and threatening than giving.'

Sometimes we give not because of the joy of giving but in order to deserve love. That way, we can have some part in creating the amount of love that comes back to us and justify it to ourselves as well. 'They love me because I cook and look after them or because I give them money.'

Just consider that for a moment. Is there anything in your life experience that suggests you might be trying to generate the amount of love that is coming your way instead of trusting that being your true self is enough? That's pretty self-destructive but it's also frighteningly common.

We can even get to the point where we will only accept the level or amount of love we feel we deserve so we actually control our lives in order to ensure we don't get more than we can handle.

Examples of limiting the amount of love that comes to you are:

♦ Having an affair with a married man/woman (very exciting but only in short bursts).

♦ Living a hermit-like life (where no one can get under your skin).

♦ Over working (so you have no time to relax and have fun).

♦ Letting people down by forgetting

appointments (so they won't appreciate your full worth).

♦ Having too many people/pets to care for (so you get love but have to work hard for it)

♦ Not encouraging your partner to help you explore your own sexuality by putting their pleasure first every time.

TRUE GIVING

Doing anything that makes us feel good is great but if that feeling requires the slightest response from another it is not true giving. It is also not true giving if you *insist* that your gift is received by a reluctant other.

Giving, in prosperity work, is only effective if it is unconditional. Yes, it does feel good to give and that's the meaning behind the saying 'virtue is its own reward.' But it's a fine line: if we give *in order* to feel good about ourselves or because we want something in return from the other, that is *not* giving; it is exchange.

There's nothing wrong with exchange (it's what money is all about) and by Law of Attraction it will give you more opportunities to experience exchange; but it must *not* be mistaken for giving.

Here are some examples of exchange that spiritual people often erroneously believe are giving:

♦ Giving a free place on a workshop (in order to fill the seats).

♦ Giving a free place on a workshop

because that person really needs the help.
(that's control and, knowing better than
they do, not giving).

♦ Giving a gift of money with a condition
on it (i.e. 'Use that for something useful/
use that to come and visit us).

♦ Giving money in order to see the look
of gratitude or relief on the other person's
face (that's a payback that gives you a
warm feeling inside).

♦ Giving time, money or energy because
you feel guilty about the other person's
situation in life (again, that's to salve your
own guilt as much as to help them).

Reading the above may make you feel quite upset
or angry. If it's any help, I have done all of the
above myself and there's *nothing wrong* with any
of them. They are certainly stages towards feeling
relief or experiencing better emotions which is
always good. They will bring you opportunities
to feel the same again by giving again but they
won't help you to harness the Law of Attraction
for increased prosperity.

Conditional giving is a deeply rooted training
issue—most of us were taught very young that
we must be generous; we must give to others; we
must share our toys; we must make sure everyone
else has a slice of cake before we take one; we
must alleviate our carbon footprint; we must
be charitable; we must be kind; we must deny
ourselves for others.

If did those things, we were rewarded with

love or, at least, approved of, and the child's ego will do almost anything for love, approval or to be noticed. The ego is our survival mechanism and it is wired to seek the attention of adults in order to be fed and taught how to fit into the tribe. Often kids of disconnected parents will refuse to give, lend or share and have a tantrum in order to get at least some kind of attention even if it's not positive. That's why there's often one 'good child' and one 'bad child' in a family; they are going to the extremes of behaviour in order to ensure that they get noticed.

So we are trained to give because we 'should' rather than because our true self wants to do so and because we get the strokes that say we are a good person.

So very often I hear people saying 'I just want to help others.' That rarely shows positive energy in the auric field, no matter what the speaker may think. It either shows up as 'I think others are in need of my help,' or it radiates, 'I need to justify my existence by helping others.' Either way, it's hard to attract prosperity when they are telling the Universe very clearly that they want It to focus on the other person (which it won't do because that would be a clear violation of free will).

Even worse, they are trying to impose a vibration on the person who they think needs help that the person in question may not be willing or able to receive. People will ask when they need help; sometimes they have to get pretty low before they will ask but that's because their pride is too strong to open up. I've been there, for sure! But once we can give up our stubbornness and pride and say 'I need help,' then we are open and receptive to the Universe and its Grace.

Kahlil Gibran says, '*Pride is taking less than you need.*' Often we give to others at the expense of ourselves because of our 'your need is greater than mine' training. Can you see how subtle that is? *Give to others and suffer willingly and you will be given your reward by God.* Prosperity just doesn't work when there is any suffering involved; if you feel suffering then you cannot attract joy.

In Louisa M. Alcott's *Little Women,* Beth gets scarlet fever from going to help a poor family who are sick. The story may be old-fashioned and promote Beth's kindness but it also shows how Beth's attention to strangers causes her and her own family great suffering. Beth also dies young. That's what happens to saints. We've looked at saints before in this book. Be warned! I say that with hand on heart as an ordained minister even though I know it may sound dreadful.

Saints are people who die young and in pain because they believe that God thinks it's appropriate for them to suffer in order to purge their souls of sin. That's not any God that I know of—or want to know. If sainthood is what you want, that's fine, but you don't need to be reading a book on prosperity!

If you want a good old-fashioned children's story about how the Law of Attraction does work through being good and kind and generous, please read *A Little Princess* by Frances Hodgson Burnett (Penguin). Sara, the heroine, makes herself happy with her imagination and shines a light of pure joy that brings her—and all her friends—prosperity. But she has to do the work for herself and appreciate all that is good in her life in order to create the life she wants before she can help others.

It gets worse before it gets better, I'm afraid. Do you give to charity? Do you do it by standing order or do you give to the *Big Issue* seller outside the supermarket because you can't walk by without feeling guilty?

Giving to charity by standing order or direct debit carries no significant energy. If you give consciously with great joy, the money is much more powerful for those on the other end of the gift and is more likely to reach those of a corresponding energy who can actually use the gift for good.

It serves them too if you can experience unconditional love when you give rather than giving with indifference or guilt. Giving to a beggar or magazine seller through guilt carries a slight negative energy which will detract—just a little— from the value of the gift. If you love *Big Issue,* that's fine, but what does it say to the Universe if you are giving money to someone for a magazine that you don't want in order to feel relief? It says, 'give me more of this experience of having to buy things I don't want in order to feel good.' It will obey you; it has to. That's the Law.

Let's go back to Jesus of Nazareth. He said, '*thou shalt love thy neighbour as yourself.*' (Matt 22:39 quoting Leviticus 19:18). He did not say, 'thou shalt love your neighbour more than yourself.'

Balance, balance, balance.

One of the reasons that I love Ho'oponopono is because it teaches that all the problems are in *us,* not *them.* We think we see someone in need so we feel the urge to help them. Did they ask? Okay, fine. Then it's our business. If not, why are we interfering in their life? If I see trouble in the world and feel unhappy about it, it's because of the imbalance in me. If I see anger and hatred and war, it is because I have anger, hatred and war in me. If I go and try and sort out that war without sorting myself out first I will just be taking more of the same energy to the trouble spot and pushing, pushing, pushing instead of attracting peace.

This is the toughest lesson of all prosperity training: let go and let God. Let the world be. Our business is not what's going on out there but what is going on in us. If we clear ourselves, 'out there' cannot impinge on us. And if we teach then others to clear themselves, nothing can impinge on them either. If that spreads, sooner or later, there can be no anger, hatred or war if we all deal with ourselves. It's baby steps, yes. But they are *real* steps, not illusory ones.

If we learn to receive, then we can teach others to receive their own prosperity. If we don't we can't. We owe the world that teaching because without it, there can be no solutions.

Think of it like filling your car with fuel before you give others a lift. If you don't take care of yourself and your car, then eventually you end up pushing them and the car to their destination and being utterly exhausted while they tell you off for making them late!

So, how does one learn the balance between giving and receiving? How does one open up to the giving abundance of the Universe?

TITHING

Every single one of my books on prosperity includes a section on tithing. This is the greatest spiritual abundance tool that there is. Tithing with money or time is a way of putting your relationship with the Source first, celebration second and *everything else* third. There's a full explanation of tithing on my blog www.totallylookedafter.blogspot.com or in *From Credit Crunch to Pure Prosperity* (O Books).

What puts most people off the idea of tithing is that it's believed to be ten per cent of your income and it's supposed to be given to a church/temple or a charity. The good news is that I've discovered through 20 years of research that it *doesn't* have to be ten per cent (although building up to ten per cent is great if and when you can) and that it should be given, consciously, to your current source of inspiration, *not* to anyone or any thing to which you are giving out of habit or because you *should*. Like any other form of giving, tithing responds with the energy given out. If you have a standing order to someone or some group then it goes out with no enthusiasm or power. If it is given consciously, then it revs up amazingly.

You have to give with no expectation of receiving but the great dichotomy is that the joy and the energy of the giving is returned to you in ever-increasing amounts.

What generally happens when we have financial issues is that we put paying the bills first and then look after any fun aspect of life *if* there is any money left. And of course, there isn't because it has all been used up on the essentials. The Law of Attraction will then just give us more of the same—more bills to put first. That is not the way to create financial security nor happiness!

Starting to tithe changes that energy. I suggest people begin by getting themselves a couple of pretty boxes or bags or, if you bank on the Internet, to open up a couple of savings accounts called 'Inspiration' and 'Celebration.'

Whenever you get money, consciously put just a little in those bags and/or those bank accounts before you do anything else.

Just putting aside 50p for inspiration and another

for celebration before paying the bills or taking care of others lets the Universe know very clearly that you are seeking a life of joy and satisfaction over one of lack and fear. Tithing was the main force that took me from debt and misery to prosperity and happiness and it is so easy to do!

Don't worry about the amounts; don't worry if there are direct debits that go out of your bank account before you can get there to move that money over; just do what you can.

One way to give to inspiration is to use that pot/account to save up for a book or a seminar that will take you closer to Spirit. Another way is to give a gift to someone who inspires you. But it must never be a payment of obligation. Don't buy a book because you should. Don't give to a guru because you were once inspired by them; it has to be a *now* thing. I once put aside a tithe to give to a teacher but by the time I saw him and could have given it to him, something had changed and he no longer inspired me. That was challenging because at the time of earning the money, I thought he was great. But you must stay in the now and not pay the past out of duty or the tithe will carry the energy of uncertainty or resentment.

I have a favourite church that I visit sometimes; it's very old—a former abbey—and has a knight's chapel where I love to sit and meditate. When I go there and feel inspired, I leave some money behind the flowers in the chapel. I don't put the money in the 'please help us to support this ancient place' box because that's a charity gift, not a tithe. Can you see the difference? I often give something separately for that box with a different energy.

Of course, my tithe money may end up in that box or anywhere else for that matter once it's

found but that isn't important. It may be picked up
and taken by someone who needs it. Where it goes
isn't my business; what is important is the energy
with which I gave it to God—the energy of love
and appreciation.

The second tithe gift is for celebration. It's
for *you*. The Bible is very clear on this point. So
once you've put some money aside or given it to a
source of inspiration, put some more aside for fun.
Nice stuff; happy stuff; flowers; chocolate; wine;
maybe even save for a holiday. But whatever, it
must be something that brings you pleasure and it
must take priority over paying bills or doing the
shopping.

In the Bible the third tithe is charity; *this was
given every third year only* and not every single
month. There were two reasons behind this. Firstly,
if everyone followed the laws of tithing, not much
charity was required. And secondly, all farmers left
what was known as the gleanings of their crops for
the poor. They would cut the grain or fruits but not
return to that field to check that they hadn't left
anything behind. Usually there were crops that had
been missed but those, then, belonged to the poor.
There's a whole section in the *Book of Ruth* about
the heroine gleaning in the fields to feed herself
and her mother-in-law.

The fourth tithe in the Bible was the Sabbath
tithe. Every seventh year, the fields were left
fallow and all debts forgiven. What a great idea!
Imagine only being able to take on a debt for
seven years. People were honour-bound to try and
repay the loan but, if they couldn't it was given
up and released so that the person had a chance
to move on and prosper. We are seeing some of
this with the forgiveness of some world debt but

more would be great. So, if someone owes you and has done for some time, consider giving them a Sabbath forgiveness because that will release both them and you. And letting go of the strain around a debt owed to you will help the Law of Attraction to bring you prosperity from another source.

Tithing works with time and attention as well. I seem to have a small farm to manage in the mornings nowadays so I make sure that I offer up a prayer of appreciation and have a handful of blueberries or some other treat before I feed dog, cat, chickens, fish and anything else that may have moved in. It's very simple but it shows the Universe my favoured order of life. I only have to forget and feed the others first and something always comes up to make it harder for me to take care of myself later in the day.

I open my computer in the morning and the emails come in, I always read the Abraham-Hicks inspirational note first, then the www.tut. com inspirational note, then any messages from friends and *only then* any work or financial emails. On some days that is still a challenge but it really makes the rest of the day flow much better.

Incidentally, don't worry if you accidentally put celebration before inspiration ... or you forget until half-way through the day. Live lightly with this; it's meant to be fun not an obligation. As mentioned earlier, I put perfume on before I light a candle at my desk in the morning because I want to be happy first and *then* inspired.

But, as with everything in this book, don't take my word for it, in fact, don't believe a word I say! I can only tell you my truth. Try it yourself — and play with it until it fits and feels good to you.

EXERCISE SIX

Find some website or book that provides you with constant inspiration. Seek out new sources of inspiration so that the old ones don't become stale.

Ensure that every morning, as you get up, you read something from it. *YouTube* has some wonderful inspirational videos. Don't compromise on requiring inspiration from the Universe and allowing yourself to receive it. This book couldn't possibly have been written without thousands of sources of inspiration. Maybe you'll be the one writing the next prosperity book?

THE SPIRITUAL LAW OF GRACE.

'*It is only when you have both divine Grace
and human endeavour that you can experience
bliss, just as you can enjoy the breeze of a fan
only when you have both a fan and the electrical
energy to operate it.*'
Sai Baba.

'*Grace is given to heal the spiritually sick, not to
decorate spiritual heroes,*'
Martin Luther.

We are extensions of Source Energy and everything is within us. But sometimes it really doesn't feel like that.

If Source is a tapestry, then we are like individual threads in that tapestry. We're an integral part of that tapestry but we are not all of it, even though we can call on different aspects within that tapestry.

If one individual life is a blue thread and another a green thread and a third a yellow thread then we can start to see that each of us has a specific rôle in the great One-ness. We can't carry out the rôle of any other colour or texture of thread than our own *but we are still a part of the whole*.

Another analogy would be that each of us is part of an organ within a great being—Kabbalah teaches that we are all divine sparks within the body of God's child, Adam Kadmon, and that we all need to perfect for the divine baby to be born. The heart is vital, as are the lungs, the liver, the

114

digestive system and the kidneys, but none of them can or should do the work of the others.

Esther Hicks has spoken of other people channeling the energy known as Abraham, saying that they can't channel exactly what she is translating because she is unique and therefore her focus with Source is unique. The others channeling may be very similar but they, too, must be unique and what they experience and channel is from their own particular connection with Source. It's no less than the Abraham channel; it's just subtly different.

So, we are It and It is us *but…*

It's a natural human need to be able to call on something bigger and more knowledgeable than ourselves in times of need, because that's what children do and nearly all the great religious teachings call us humans 'Children of God.'

I'm perfectly happy with the idea that it's up to us to move in the direction of our happiness and that if we do that, the Universe bends over backwards to help us. But sometimes we just need help.

If I am in any trouble then I want to say 'Please help me!'

Grace is defined as 'a gift from God' in the New Testament. The word used is *charis* which means joy, pleasure, delight, good will, loving kindness, happiness and a whole host of other good things. It's supposed to be different from mercy which is where we are treated with kindness when we don't deserve it. Grace has nothing to do with whether or not we are worthy; it just comes. And it is nearly always totally unexpected.

But if Grace exists, why doesn't it come more often? This is where I can tie it in with the Law of Attraction in that it comes when we ask for help or when we simply give up. Once we give up, we stop resisting our good.

In Kabbalistic terms, Grace comes when we have lined ourselves up in balance on the central column of the Tree of Life, rather than being over-active or over-analytical on the side pillars.

When we are balanced or centred, we open up. Opening up both offers and surrenders the issue. It takes it away from our ego and away from our false pride and allows access to all the love that we have been unconsciously pushing away through trying to control things.

Abraham-Hicks would say it is the process of stopping rowing against the river and the peace of letting our good flow to us. It's allowing.

And if the Law of Attraction is all-encompassing then, if we truly believe that there is a greater power that will help us, surely that must become true even if it wasn't true to start with. After all, a belief is just a repeated thought and for century after century, humanity has believed in God, gods, angels and elemental powers.

In the modern world where people don't like or approve of 'God' we have angels instead. But angels, like the Hindu gods, are aspects of the Divine and must be dealt with accordingly. If we make just one angel our muse then we are blocking ourselves off from the Source. It's a tricky one because the first time we turn to an angelic energy, we may well receive the blessing of Grace—because we have let go of control. The secret is not to make that angel a god because then it becomes a blocking factor, not an essence of assistance.

Angels are a different aspect of the same tapestry. Perhaps we are the warp and they are the woof. If we are the heart, they are the blood. But the ancient mystical traditions are emphatic about angels: they are created from the World of Spirit whereas we humans are created from the World of Divinity. We are children of the Source; angels are servants of the source. While it's a good idea to ask for guidance from a servant, it only has one particular line of expertise and it's inappropriate to ask one to do a task which is outside its remit. .

A good way of looking at angels being integral to the whole inclusive scheme of things is to look at the psychological idea of archetypes. Carl Jung is the best-known of those who have defined the specific characteristics that are within us. He wrote of the Anima (perfect feminine), and Animus (perfect masculine) and several other aspects that we all contain within ourselves. These include:

♦ The father/priest.

♦ The mother/priestess.

♦ The hero/warrior.

♦ The maiden.

♦ The wise old man/woman.

♦ The magician or king.

♦ The trickster.

♦ The witch, temptress or sorceress (a more politically correct translation would be 'the sexual woman!').

All of these equate to the Greek, Roman, Hindu

and Norse gods and to the attributes of the planets of the Solar system.

♦ Father: Sun

♦ Mother: Earth

♦ Hero: Mars

♦ Maiden: Moon

♦ Wise person: Saturn

♦ Trickster: Mercury

♦ Temptress: Venus

♦ King: Jupiter

The Western gods all have a particular day assigned to them and although Earth does not have a specific day; she had her own goddess, Ceres, now often called Gaia.

♦ Sun—Sunday (Apollo/Helios in Graeco-Roman, Balder in Norse)

♦ Moon—Monday (Diana/Artemis/Frigga)

♦ Mars—Tuesday (Mars/Ares/Athene/Tyr)

♦ Mercury—Wednesday (Mercury/Hermes/Woden)

♦ Jupiter—Thursday (Jupiter/Zeus/Thor)

♦ Venus—Friday   (Venus/Aphrodite/
Freya)

♦ Saturn—Saturday (Saturn/the Noms—
Fates)

You may notice that the planets Uranus, Neptune and Pluto/Kuyper Belt are excluded. This is because they are not visible to the naked eye and these correspondences were developed before we had the ability to discern their presence.

In exact parallel we have the best-known teaching Archangels.

♦ Sunday—Michael

♦ Monday—Gabriel

♦ Tuesday—Khamael/Samael

♦ Wednesday—Raphael

♦ Thursday—Zadkiel/Sachiel*

♦ Friday—Haniel

♦ Saturday—Cassiel

Each of the days, gods and archangels have been imbued with particular characteristics since the dawn of time and these are still acknowledged by both magical practitioners and angelologists. Whether or not this has always been true, it has been believed for so long that it has become true:

♦ Sunday/Michael: leadership, priesthood, true ambition, marriage.

♦ Monday/Gabriel: family, home, prophecy, childbirth.

♦ Tuesday/Khamael: protection, conflict, competition, sports, bravery, honour

♦ Wednesday/Raphael: Education, the arts, the intellect, communication, music, writing, divination, psychic abilities, poetry, healing.

♦ Thursday/Zadkiel: Money, commerce, employment, opportunity, prosperity, material wealth, justice.

♦ Friday/Haniel: Love, sexuality, ecstasy, peace, fertility, creativity.

♦ Saturday/Cassiel: Endings, old age, structures, karma.

All these attributes are within us somewhere. Most of them are unknown and unacknowledged and we feel somehow lacking in that sphere. It's a lot easier to contact an angel of prosperity when we're feeling broke than it is to pray to God (who we fear may blame us for doing something 'wrong') or to tune into our own, hidden, inner King or Queen archetype. After all, if we were feeling like royalty we would be unlikely to be feeling broke.

Each of us leans towards one or two primary archetypes and is comfortable in that sphere. I don't often call on the energy of Raphael because

I adore writing and communicating and practising as a healer so I don't feel any lack in that respect. But I have been known to call on the energy of Michael and Zadkiel to promote success and right livelihood for me as a writer and communicator because I used to be less sure of myself when it comes to promotion. And I'm a big fan of Khamael/Samael because I've been learning slowly and steadily over the years the value of boundaries.

I would suggest that an angelic being is a channel of Grace for the times when we are not vibrationally a match to our own Source energy. The Western Mystical and Alchemical traditions are clear that what we refer to as an angel is not a human being (although as the word 'angel' means 'messenger' a human can act like an angel. The differences are two-fold:

♦ An angel does not have free will in the way we do

♦ An angel has paranormal powers that we don't.

Angels and free will is always a challenging question when I talk on angels to people involved in the New Age because we do get caught up in the idea of anthropomorphism and 'see' angels as human figures. They have been depicted as humanoid in religious art for so many centuries that it's unusual for them to be shown any other way. But that is just another very useful example of how programmed we are by religion, whether we realise it or not.

An angel is a source of spiritual energy which is not, and never has been, incarnate. It is a being which is totally focused on its one job. The human heart can't decide that it's going to double as the liver or fill in for the brain; it just acts like a heart. So an angel is complete being just one aspect of the divine where we humans can be many aspects. We can decide whether or not to eat or talk or go to work and, if set a particular task, will need to stop now and then for refreshment and relief. An angel never varies from one hundred per cent focus on its job.

So there is no point in asking Raphael for money; he doesn't *do* money. That's Zadkiel There's no point in asking Haniel for protection because she doesn't *do* protection. That's Khamael/Samael. And there is no point in trying to adopt an archangel as your guardian angel because archangels aren't guardian angels. A guardian angel is an angel whose sole job is to protect you from harm; not to promote your career or help your relationship with your mother. If you have a particular fondness for one of the archangelic energies it's most likely that they resonate with your astrological Sun or Moon sign.

The archangels do have a wider remit than the angels and each angel works to a particular archangel. When we invoke an archangel, that request is passed to the Source and the reply is passed back to that archangel which deputes an angel to pass it on to us from an angel. It's very logical; not for nothing are the angelic hosts called 'Heaven's Civil Service.'

Although many modern angel teachers imply that we humans deal directly with archangels, the ancient teachers emphasise that this is simply not so. The average archangel is, energetically, the size of a sun. We receive the essence of that archangel through one of its angels. In that way we get direct contact between us and the archangel and via it to the Source instead of having to share the whole archangelic energy with everyone else.

You may have noticed earlier on that I wrote that Khamael/Samael is the angelic energy to call on for protection. Most modern teachers call on Michael. This will work because Michael's remit includes you life's path and soul's destiny. Therefore his angels are empowered to help you move to your right place in life. If you are in trouble or danger you are clearly in the wrong place and assistance may be offered. It is quite possible to carry 'the sword of Michael' before you as a protective device. This will ward off all energies which are not part of your life's path.

However, the angelic presence to invoke if you are in serious danger or if you have dropped your energy enough to be threatened by enemies, whether psychologically or physically, is the angel of Mars. This is the great warrior and hero. He is very unpopular with angelologists because he has long been associated with Satan and all that is evil. This is because of a textual interpretation of the name Samael, sometimes spelt with what looks to us like a C or K and sometimes with what looks like an S. Because of the confusion (and you don't want to be worrying about whether you're calling a frightening energy!) it's easier to invoke the energy of Khamael.

Samael is the Archangel of destruction. That means that he breaks down substances, thoughts and feelings which are negative. It is an aspect of Samael that causes leaves and dead bodies to rot so that they can become the earth that will nurture and support the next year's growth. Samael breaks relationships; destroys cities; rules surgery, brings a swift death if suffering is terminal. He is scary and he is powerful.

If you ever saw the TV series *Torchwood: Children of Earth* and remember the denouement where Captain Jack had to make a great sacrifice to save the world, that's the best definition you can have of the energy of Samael.

It's because of this frightening aspect that Samael was given the two names: Khamiel for the 'good guy' aspect and Samael for the 'bad guy' aspect. So surgery would come under Khamiel if it worked and Samael if it didn't. Never mind the fact that the patient's life path was that he was meant to die at that time and in that way.

If everything is One then there is no source of evil apart from human decisions. Therefore there cannot be a demonic presence in the angelic hosts. There can certainly be violent, powerful and destructive elements but these are not to be seen as 'bad.'

The devil is basically a Christian invention to scare people into being good. There have long been dark gods and Bodhisattvas such as Anubis, Hades, Kali and Ekajati and humanity needs duality in faith because we live in a world of dark and light. But the devil was based on the Pagan god Pan who had goat's feet and horns on his head. Pan was very powerful and the new faith had to demonise him to help people move away.

So what has this to do with the Spiritual Law of Grace? The angels have come back into fashion to help us seek help where we are frightened of prayer to a God we may perceive as judgmental, cruel or simply ineffective. If we turn our attention just one iota towards hope and love we are aligned with the possibility of Grace.

How we use the angelic energies to support and guide us and bring us to Grace is simple. We consider which of the angelic/archetypal energies is the one we need to bring us into alignment (and you'll never go wrong with Michael in that respect!) and you invoke for the power of that angel *in you*.

'Power of Zadkiel *in me*' means that you are calling for balance and fullness in you in the area of abundance or justice. 'Power of Raphael *in me*' means you are calling for balance and fullness in you in the area of healing or communication.

In the ancient teachings, an archangelic energy is invoked through writing to it in a mystical language in certain colours and in certain styles on the appropriate day. This is because doing so draws the archetype of that archangelic being into your own psyche. It makes the angel's energy one with yours so that you can become are lined up and Grace can be experienced.

In this way, we keep the first commandment; we ask for the angels' assistance in contacting the Source rather than making the assistance itself our total focus.

So, whenever you feel that you need some support, you aren't confident that you're aligned and your earthly best friend's not available, see which if the angelic energies seems to offer the most comfort. Ask for that angel's help in drawing down the love of the Source to assist you in bringing you back to balance

Then comes inspiration; guidance and Grace.

So, prosperity seeker, ask, believing—and it is given.

ACKNOWLEDGEMENTS

With thanks and acknowledgement to:

Peter Dickinson
Adam Simmonds
Sheila Minifie
Barbara Palmer
David Goddard www.davidgoddard.com
Gerry and Esther Hicks www.abraham-hicks.com
Mike Dooley www.tut.com
Barbara Winter www.joyfullyjobless.com
Eckhart Tolle www.eckhardtolle.com
Byron Katie www.thework.com
Z'ev ben Shimon Halevi www.kabbalahsociety.org

You can find Maggy Whitehouse on:

www.pureprosperity.com
www.treeofsapphires.com
www.totallylookedafter.blogspot.com
www.facebook.com/maggy.whitehouse
www.twitter.com/maggywhitehouse